Front Jacket
Parkhouse Hill and Chrome Hill
(WTP, Walk 28, June 22)
Previous Page
Monet-esque footbridge at Barber Booth
(Walk 12, Dec 23)
This Frontispiece
In upper Ramsden Clough
(Walk 5, Aug 23)
Title Page Right
Guide Stoop on Beeley Moor
(Walk 46, Sept 25)

Walk The Peak 2

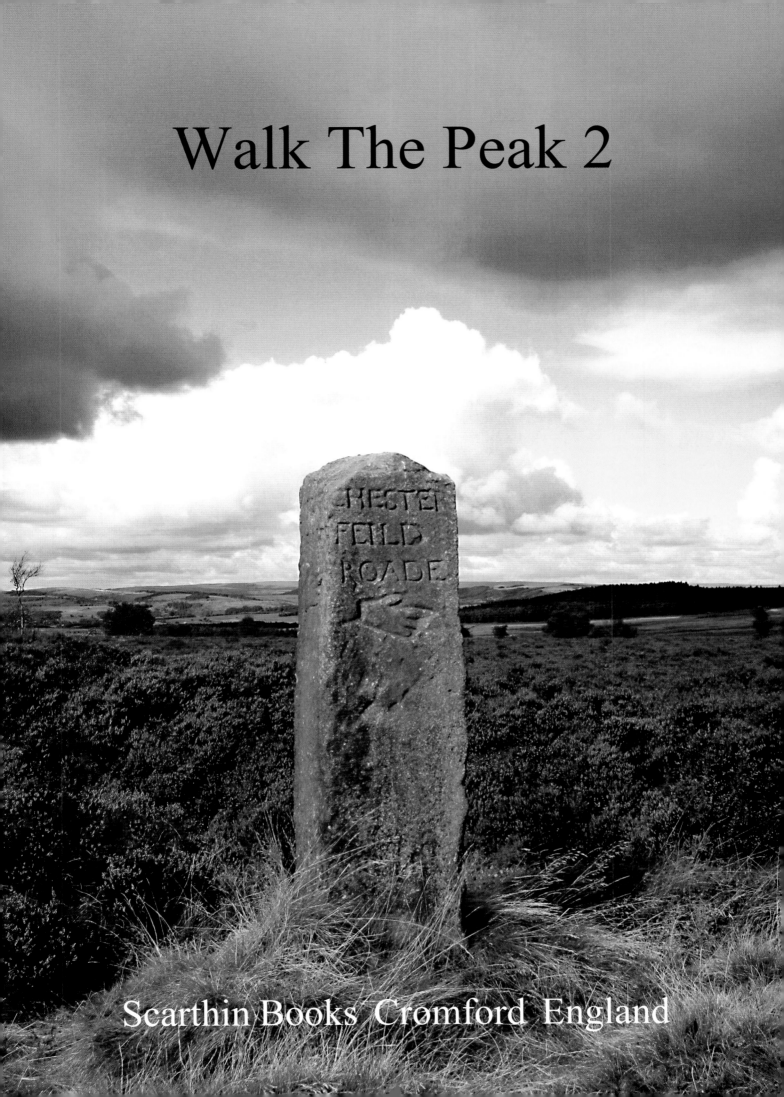

Scarthin Books Cromford England

Canyards Hills (Walk 18, Oct 24)

Scarthin Books, Cromford,
Derbyshire DE4 3QF, UK. (01629 823272)
www.scarthinbooks.com

Printed in China by 1010 Printing
International Ltd

A CIP catalogue record for this book
is available from the British Library

Walk The Peak 2
Copyright © Rod Dunn, 2011

ISBN 9781900446143

Disclaimer
Like most outdoor activities, walking and scrambling can be hazardous and are done entirely at your own risk. As well as the terrain, other dangers may include the weather; animals; landslip; rock-fall; quarry and mine workings; ordnance ammunition; outdoor pursuits participants and their equipment, and road and off-road vehicles. The publisher, the author or the landowner(s) are not liable for any injuries or loss of life to first or third parties or responsible for the loss or damage to first or third person property or equipment or losing one's direction and incurring any discomfort or expense whatsoever whilst on any of the walks in this publication or taking any of the advice or acting on other information contained so herein.

Always err on the side of caution. The dales, hills and crags will be there for another day - make sure you are.

In An Emergency
Dial 999 and ask for police and mountain rescue. Give your location as exactly as possible together with the suspected injuries of the casualty. If phoning from a mobile, keep the phone switched on. See also page 18.

Note The ozone layer over northern Europe is now much depleted and skin cancer is on the increase. If you're going to be outside for extended periods cover up and use sunblock.

Wardlow Hay Cop (right), seen from Walk 43, is now on access land (see p.230)

Map of The Peak District National Park (and environs)

north

Marsden •

• Holmfirth

Wessenden Moor

Black Hill

• Penistone

Crowden •

Longdendale

Langsett •

Greater Manchester

Torrs Gorge Millennium Walkway

Pike Lowe

Bleaklow

Upper Derwent

Glossop •

Alport Castles

Bradfield •

Kinder Scout

The Downfall

Stanage Edge

• Sheffield

Hayfield •

Lyme Park

• Edale

The Great Ridge

Walks on Dark Peak Map

White Nancy

Eldon Hole •

• Castleton

Carl Wark

Walks on White Peak Map

• Eyam

Goyt Valley

Buxton •

Cressbrook Dale

Coombs Dale

Eastern Edges

• Macclesfield

Chee Dale •

Shutlingsloe

Chrome Hill

• *Five Wells*

Chatsworth •

Chesterfield •

• Bakewell

Longnor •

Lathkill Dale

The Roaches

• *Arbor Low*

Nine Ladies

Pilsbury Castle •

Mermaid (PH) •

• Hartington

• Matlock

• Leek

High Tor   *Crich Stand* •

Combes Valley

Minning Low •

Cromford •

Thors Cave

Manifold Valley

Dovedale

Brassington •

Alport Stone •

Ilam Rock

Carsington Water

Cromford Canal

I———————I

0   16 kms
                     10 miles

Thorpe •

• Ashbourne

Contents

Map of Area ... *page 5*
Location of Walks ... *page 8*
Introduction ... *page 9*
Book Information ... *page 18*
Key To Maps ... *page 19*

Wild primroses at Lower Fleetgreen (Walk 33, May 8)

Derwent Reservoir and its eastern dam tower in the autumn (Walk 19, Nov 15)

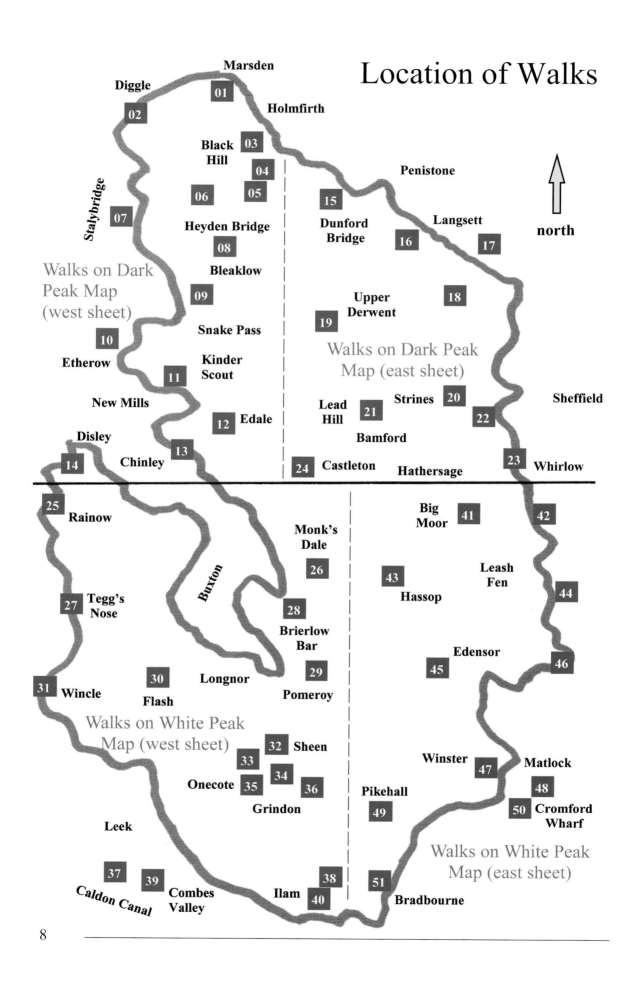

Location of Walks

Marsden
Diggle
01
Holmfirth
02
Black
Hill
03
04
Penistone
06
05
15
Stalybridge
07
Heyden Bridge
Dunford
Bridge
Langsett
16
17
08
Bleaklow
Walks on Dark
Peak Map
(west sheet)
09
18
Upper
Derwent
19
Snake Pass
Walks on Dark Peak
Map (east sheet)
10
Kinder
Scout
Etherow
11
New Mills
Strines
Sheffield
Lead
Hill
20
Disley
12
Edale
21
22
Chinley
13
Bamford
14
24
Castleton
Hathersage
23
Whirlow
25
Rainow
Big
Moor
41
42
Monk's
Dale
27
Tegg's
Nose
26
Buxton
43
Leash
Fen
Hassop
44
28
Brierlow
Bar
30
Longnor
29
Edensor
46
31
Wincle
Flash
Pomeroy
45
Walks on White Peak
Map (west sheet)
32
Sheen
33
Winster
Matlock
34
47
Onecote
35
36
48
Pikehall
Grindon
50
Cromford
Wharf
49
Leek
Walks on White Peak
Map (east sheet)
37
39
Combes
Valley
38
51
Caldon Canal
Ilam
40
Bradbourne

north

8

Introduction

Following the publication of *Walk The Peak* in 2007, I was asked by a number of walkers whether it would be possible for me to produce a second volume of walks in the Peak District. After some research, I concluded that it would indeed be possible to describe another 50 walks of equal stature and interest as those had in *Walk The Peak* (*WTP*). As I already had a few routes and photos trimmed from *WTP* and retained the *Publisher* templates, the project was soon underway. As per *WTP*, all the walks are to be found on the O/S 1 : 25 000 *Explorer* series for the Dark and White Peak Areas. If you also do all 100 walks in the reverse direction than described, the new vistas seen would be as though you were on 100 different walks altogether!

The format is similar to the first volume, with a few aircraft wrecks visited; the wildlife noted as we walked the routes; some Neolithic sites, caves and carvings met, but most important are the rambles themselves through this unique and ecologically fragile countryside. There's a shorter pictorial Introduction this time, with a few topics not covered in *Walk The Peak*.

If, at the end of perusing both volumes you breathe a huge sigh of relief because I haven't included your own favourite haunt, then that's the way it should be. So wherever it is, always treasure your own personal ...

... gateway to freedom.

White Peak Scenery The carboniferous limestone in the White Peak has been dissolved, eroded and folded into diverse landscapes. Rivers have cut deep into the limestone plateau forming gorges such as Dove Dale and Chee Dale. **Top.** *Upper Lathkill Dale. Typical of such dales, it has contrasting flora on the north and south facing slopes.* **Bottom.** *A week or so either side of St George's Day on April 23, the edible St George's mushroom may be seen in rings amidst the grasses of such dales as Cressbrook (May 2).*

Tissington Spires, Dove Dale **Inset**. *Burnet rose in Deep Dale (Walk 28, June 17)*

A caver high up on Windy Ledge at Stoney Middleton Crags on the way to Ivy Green Cave. The pillar is the Tower of Babel, with climbing routes "Sin" and "Glory Road".

Dark Peak Scenery Burnt, overgrazed and eroded by acid rain and ferocious weather, the scenery of the Dark Peak blanket bogs and heather moors can be both stark and beautiful. The peat, formed by the decomposition of *Sphagnum* moss over a period of about 5,000 years, is rapidly being blown away in many places and urgent conservation is under way by planting cotton-grass and wavy hair-grass, and seeding with heather cuttings. **Top.** *Yorkshire flagstones are being laid on many boggy paths to reduce erosion caused by walkers, such as this example leading to Black Hill summit (Walk 2).* **Bottom.** *The exposed Grinah Stones east of Bleaklow Hill show the scars of an elemental battering.*

The high blanket bogs and moors have been dissected over the millennia by watercourses forming gullies and deep valleys called cloughs. These are most prominent on the flanks of Kinder Scout and Bleaklow. **Top.** *Looking to Crowden Great Brook from Wild Boar Clough, Bleaklow.* **Bottom.** *A temperature inversion beneath The Great Ridge above Castleton. Left is the east-facing wall of Mam Tor showing the strata of shale, grit and shale-grits responsible for the landslips in the Dark Peak, including Alport Castles.*

Bridleway Concerns Top. *Road 4x4 vehicles and motocross bikes jostle for position at the top of the hugely eroded track of Chapel Gate. Walkers? Well, we just give way! (Walk 12, Dec 13).* Mountain-bikers are also causing damage to some bridleways and public footpaths. One of the reasons is that most cyclists do not follow the ruts made by their fellow cyclists, but forge a new passage through easier terrain, thus ever widening the bridleway. **Below.** *The path from Cutthroat Bridge to Whinstone Lee Tor (Walk 21, Nov 12) is now a mud-bath 8 metres wide in places. To make a circuit of the route, some bikers illegally descend Lead Hill on the public footpath, thus damaging this path, too.*

Styles of Stiles (All met on walks in this book)

Wall step-stile

Conventional, user-friendly type

Squeezer-stile (some are even narrower!)

A confuse-the-walker stile

Lonely stile

Ladder stile

Walking on a compass bearing using a *Silva* Compass

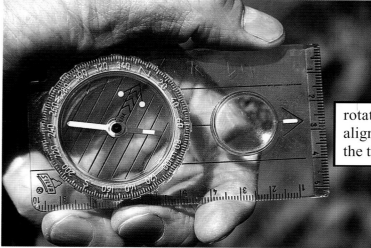

To walk in the correct direction on a given bearing, first set the bearing, in this example 60°, on the numbered dial.

rotate the bezel with your hand to align the bearing with the direction of the travel arrow on the compass base.

Ensure that there are no metal objects close to the compass.

Hold the compass level in your hand and rotate your body until the red needle lines up with the north arrow inside the bezel, then :

← walk in the direction this arrow, the direction of travel arrow, points to.

There is, of course, much more to navigation than this simple exercise. There is no substitute for experience and most outdoor clothing and equipment shops also stock booklets on map reading and navigation. Global Positioning System (GPS) personal navigators also have similar functions, but always take a map/compass as back-up as batteries can fail and fluctuating solar radiation has been known to give inaccurate readings on occasions.

Navigation skills are essential when fog, mist or low cloud descends. Under such conditions, even huge features such as The Wheel Stones on Derwent Edge (Walk The Peak, Walk 16, page 101) **Above***, only appear when you are a few metres away from them.*

Grid References

We are fortunate that all of Great Britain has been extensively mapped and that there is a
1 : 25 000 *Explorer* series of Ordnance Survey maps for all of England, Scotland and Wales.
The countries have been split up into a grid system so that a unique reference can be
determined for any point or feature on the maps and hence any position on the ground.

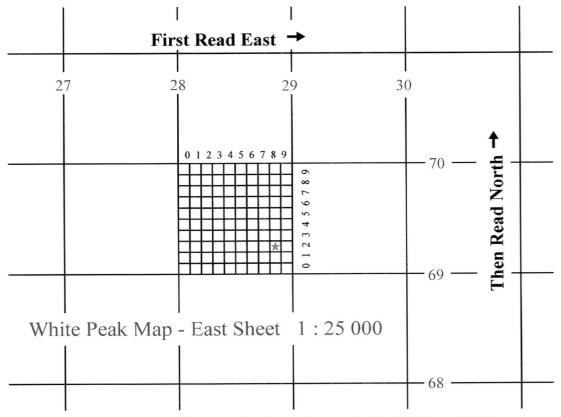

First Read East →

Then Read North ↑

White Peak Map - East Sheet   1 : 25 000

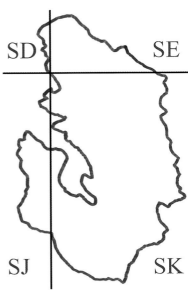

SD   SE

SJ   SK

The countries have been sub-divided into 100 km squares;
10 km squares and the 1 km squares that appear on the
Explorer maps. The 1 km squares are numbered from 00 to 99
both across (eastings) and up (northings) the page, starting
from a 100 km datum. This means that every 100 kms the 1 km
numbers are repeated. To give a unique reference, the
corners of the maps show the 100 km squares as small
numbers. To avoid the confusion of too many numbers, a letter
system also operates for the 100 km squares. These are at the
corners of each map and also where a new 100 km square
starts. Viewing the map left it can be seen that the Peak District
has parts of four 100 km squares. Using an O/S or *Silva*
romer or by marking the divisions on paper from the map
edges the 1 km squares can be further divided into 100 metre
squares. Thus, the unique grid ref for the red star is SK 288
692 and, on the *White Peak* map, it is the tourist attraction
blue star for the tumulus on Beeley Moor (met on Walk 46!).

Book Information

To complement this book, O/S *Explorer* maps Nos. OL1 and OL24 are required for map and compass work and general map reading. No walks overlap maps, so you only ever need one map. Better still, photocopy or scan and print the relevant area together with the route directions, and back to back them in a plastic A4 envelope. Use highlighter/pen to transcribe route/features from sketch maps to the O/S section. Most sketch maps contain information not on the O/S maps. Weatherproof the top with sticky tape. Software such as *TrackLogs Digital Mapping* can enable the printing of larger scales. On wild walks, include sufficient area for an escape route. All the sketch maps and route descriptions in the book are presented on adjacent pages for ease of reference. Words in **bold** in the route descriptions refer to features on the sketch maps and to many reference points on the ground. Likewise, many of the photos also serve this purpose. Spelling throughout the book follows the O/S maps. The walks are described from north to south throughout The Peak. This does mean that some of the harder walks appear first, but it is the logical way to list them. As both *The Dark Peak* and *The White Peak* maps each have a west and east sheet, there are, in effect, four sections to the book - see page 8 for **Location of Walks**.

Times and Grades

Times and grades are not given as they are too subjective. Most walkers average about 3 kms (1.88 miles) per hour during a walk. Add some time on for breaks. Determine your own capabilities on the shorter walks first. There is no substitute for experience so learn your trade. An early start should ensure a car space at the most popular venues (better for seeing wildlife, too). Public transport times/routes constantly change, but some are listed. See also **www.traveline.org.uk** (page 246).

Equipment (Supplementary to that in *Walk The Peak*)

Walking Trainers are becoming fashionable but offer little or no ankle support. My daughter wears them because they're "cool" but will probably change her opinion of them after her first sprained ankle (or worse). **Personal Navigation Systems** using GPS (Global Positioning System) via satellite tracking are becoming ever more elaborate and it seems that every month new software offers more features. Unless we are careful, walkers will fall into the trap that all such paraphernalia is essential and "digital walking" will be just around the corner. There is nothing wrong with a basic GPS system to determine your position and aid navigation but do we really need digital mapping on smart phones? I thought the idea was to leave the PC at home and go for a mind-cleansing breath of fresh air. But some systems such as *SPOT* could be beneficial in an emergency if mobiles have no signal. The device sends a GPS location and messages to family/friends/emergency services via satellite (www.findmespot.com). However, you are never 100% safe in the countryside, whatever gizmos you have. **Mapping Software** enables waterproof O/S maps to be printed at home but is expensive unless you are going walkabout nationwide, in which case it is cheaper than buying all the traditional maps. **LED Headlights** are now quite powerful and lamps such as the Petzyl Myo XP or Tikka XP function well.

A basic GPS navigator

Key To Sketch Maps

▬▬▬▬▬	*A roads*	🏛	*Stately home*
﹏﹏	*B roads, minor and unclassified roads*	✳	*Point of interest*
⌒⌒	*River, canal or stream*	▲	*Youth hostel*
◯	*Reservoir, lake or pond*	✛	*Aircraft wreck*
▬▬▬	*Railway line*	✝	*War memorial*
		Pennine Way	*Named path*
⟓	*O/S altitude benchmark*	**P**	*Car park/start and finish of walk*

‐ ‐ ‐ ‐ ‐ ‐   *Public footpath, bridleway or track marked on O/S map*

‒ ‒ ‒ ‒ ‒   *Concession or other path/track or route across open country not necessarily marked on O/S map*

▲ *Triangulation (trig) pillar, toposcope or other summit feature*

→ *Route direction*   260° → *Compass bearing across open country or access land*

Note *The representation on the maps of any path, track or road or route across open country and access land is no evidence of the existence of a right of way. Stiles have a habit of becoming gates etc and the walker should be aware of this in the* **Route** *data. Access Land may be closed during grouse shooting. Phone for details : 0845 100 3298*

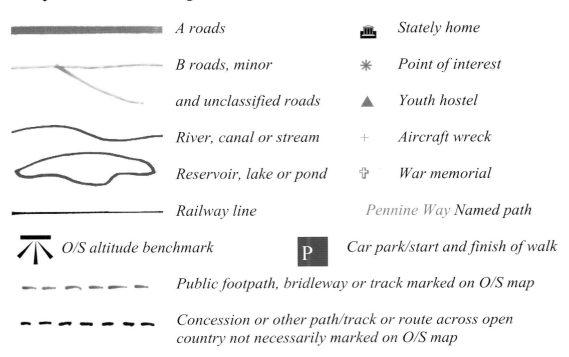

The maps in this book are all to scale and the routes can easily be transcribed onto the two required O/S maps using a highlighter pen. But you won't find the above view on the OL 24 map in The Peak as it's in the Yorkshire Dales!

Waymark Colour Codes

 Concession path

Public footpath

Public bridleway

The access land symbol together with public footpath waymark sign.

Walks On Dark Peak Map ——————— West Sheet
(Explorer Outdoor Leisure Series No 01)

The Macclesfield Canal between the Trading Post and Adlington Basin (Walk 14, Oct 8)

01 Wessenden Head, Magdalen, Royd Edge, West Nab and Scope Moss

On the way from the trig pillar on West Nab to the Fortress site on Scope Moss (Nov 9)

Our journey south starts with a path then track to see mysteriously grooved slabs on an ancient quarry-way; girdles enticing Magdalen Clough; rises to a viewpoint at West Nab then heads off-path to an aircraft wreck and an optional trek to a high-level return leg.

Length 13 kms / 8.13 miles **Map** O/S Explorer OL1, *Dark Peak Area*, West Sheet
Start/Finish Lay-bys on both sides of the A635 at Wessenden Head (SE 076 072)
Refreshments Mobile snack-bar at the lay-by; Meltham, pubs etc (1km round detour)
Terrain A mixture of easy to follow tracks and paths together with a kilometre of offpath moor to find the *Fortress* site. This is followed by a further km off-path to link up with the high-level path above Wessenden Reservoir. On this section there are signs with "Rifle range/Live firing when red flags hoisted". In many trips we have never encountered shooting but there may be! With this in mind, you may wish to return to West Nab by the same route then follow Wessenden Head Road back to the A635.

When To Go/What's There Wreckage of the *Fortress* B-17G-65 which crashed on Scope Moss in April 1945 can be found at SE 07076 09538 (GPS ref acc 5m). The crew of 5 survived; some with serious injuries. On the way there is a fine natural shelter on the east side of the Wicken Stones. An ancient wood is passed on the way to the grooved slabs on Springs Road. By the path to West Nab is an unusually christened boulder - especially if it is winter! Upland wildlife includes mountain hare, curlew and red grouse. Magdalen Clough is a heathery delight late summer and, on a further visit, you may wish to ascend to Royd Edge via the footpath running SW up tempting Royd Edge Clough to the bridleway to Sun Royd (see O/S map). A seat at the end of Royd Edge provides a fine viewpoint.

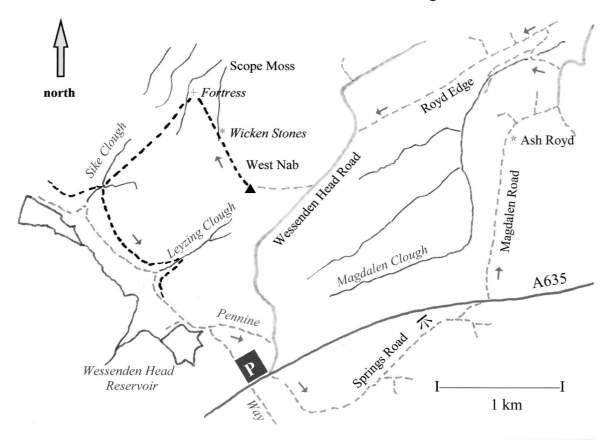

Wreckage of the Fortress as of November 2009

Route From the lay-by go over the most easterly ladder-stile. The path heads down the moor then bears left and splits to run either side of a boggy area. The right one is most used but both meet at the head of a small clough, which is rounded to a gate. On to a ladder-stile. Over, bear left up the track, passing an interesting old quarry and then the unique, grooved slabs of **Springs Road** up to a gate and the A635. Turn right. After about 40m carefully cross the road; go through the gate and walk up the bridleway, which is **Magdalen Road**. Through another gate the path runs downhill to a gate and the farm track at **Ash Royd**, noting the "Bus Stop" here and ancient wall on the left. Continue down and bear left at junction and down the lane until, at a right bend, there is a seat, footpath sign and entrance to **Royd Wood** on the left. Don't enter wood, but go down track, pass building and follow path down to footbridge. Cross and bear right, up to kissing gate. Keep ahead up cobbles and then road to T-junction. Turn left on the *Meltham Way* and follow the track up. The *Meltham Way* eventually turns right (seats) but you continue ahead on the path above **Royd Edge** to the entrance to **Sun Royd** (seat). Here, bear right, go over two stiles and follow path over field. Two more gates are met before the path rises to **Wessenden Head Road**. Turn left. After about ½ km cross the road and walk up the path to the trig pillar on **West Nab**. Now set compass to 330° and head down the moor, off-path. The slabby *Wicken Stones* are passed and about 300m later, the wreckage of the *Fortress* is reached on **Scope Moss**. Now set compass to 228° and in about a km you should reach the footbridge and path at the bottom of *Sike Clough*. Turn left and follow the path which later falls to join the *Pennine Way*. This rises to **Wessenden Head Road** where you turn right to the lay-by.

West Nab from Wessenden Head Road **Inset.** *Green-veined white at Magdalen (Aug 15)*

Purple moor-grass in autumn on Scope Moss **Inset.** *In the Wicken Stones bivvy (Nov 9)*

The unusual grooved slabs on the track of Springs Road (Aug 15)

02 Huddersfield Narrow Canal, Pots & Pans Stone and Broadstone Hill

Starting the walk by the flight of locks at Diggle (May 24)

This walk full of natural and man-made interest and fine aerial views starts beside the flight of locks at Diggle on the Huddersfield Narrow Canal; rises to St Chad's Church and beneath Primrose Hill to a towering war memorial and rock sculptures. A trek over the moor leads to Sykes Pillar on Broadstone Hill and more views from Ravenstone Brow.

Length 13 kms / 8.13 miles **Map** O/S Explorer OL1, *Dark Peak Area*, West Sheet **Start/Finish** Sam Road car park in Diggle, 3 kms north of Uppermill at SE 006 079. Uppermill is well-served with buses from Oldham, Huddersfield and Manchester areas. No 184 from Uppermill stops at Station Road, Sam Road. Trains stop at nearby Greenfield. Local rail and bus times : 0161-228-7811. Uppermill TI : 01457-87409 **Terrain** A canal towpath; farmland and moorland paths. Some lanes and off-path moor. **Refreshments** 3 pubs on route; Diggle chippy (not Sat/Sun!); Uppermill many outlets. **When To Go/What's There** This tough walk starts at Standedge Tunnel, the highest and longest canal tunnel (3¼ miles) in England. The tunnel gates portray the "leggers" who used to propel the boats through the tunnel by "walking" on the roof of the tunnel in near darkness. The towpath has an intriguing game with rotary dice! Turning areas have matured into angling pools. There is art in a tunnel. The *Pots and Pans Stone*; *Sugar Loaf* and *Shaw Rocks* on the high plateau are natural art. The giant war obelisk can be seen from miles around. Two fine canal-side buttercup meadows support lapwings late May/ June. Other wildlife includes brown hare, curlew, skylark, foxglove and on sunny days dragonflies at the pond up to St Chad's Church, which has seats and stocks. Nearby is the *Church Inn*. The pub sign announces the "Taylor family, purveyors of mental distortion since 1981". Well, we did see peacocks there once (on the way out). Honestly. This is not a walk for foggy conditions as there are edges and quarry faces with sheer drops.

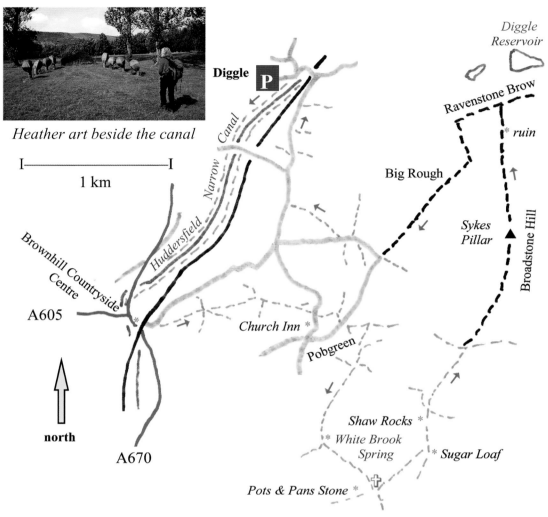

Heather art beside the canal

I————————I
1 km

north

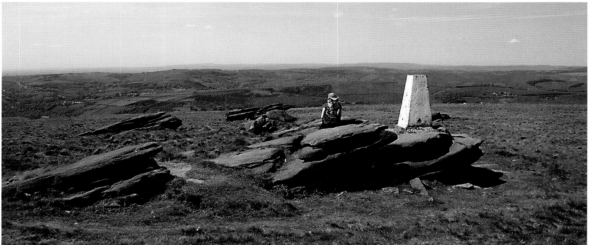

Soaking up the solitude at Sykes Pillar (May 24). Did you know that classic rock legends Barclay James Harvest lived in Diggle during their most creative years and even composed some of their music on these moors? Perhaps "Galadriel" was born up here!

Route Inside the car park, walk south to the canal towpath which leads to road (pub up to left). Cross. Onwards, pass the locks. After the art under Bridge 71 you are diverted through a car park. As path splits, take left fork and go under Bridge 73. Immediately after, turn left into the Brownhill Countryside Centre (PCs, drinks). Cross the **A670** and bear right up **Brownhill Lane**. After 100m, as the lane turns 90° left, go ahead up narrower lane and then take the footpath off to the right. It is narrow but leads to a lane. Keep ahead at fork and go through stile onto pleasant path with views. Keep left as path splits to reach two stiles. Go ahead through wall stile to another stone stile then through 3 stones and over stile. Path crosses stream and another stile leads to a fork. Go right up shady path to church. Turn right and then left past entrance gates and on up path ahead to gate and ahead through *Ivy Bank Farm*. Bear right up drive to a road. Cross, go over stile and steeply up sunken path to stile. Over, turn right on track to buildings and lane at **Pobgreen**. Go right then immediately left. Pass cottages (inc *Primrose Cottage*) on left and follow path ahead. Go over 4 stiles/rough land and *White Brook Spring* with "farm" below and stile. Don't go over but stay on path above which angles left up past pylon; crosses "track"; becomes sunken path; passes quarry face on left and rises to the *war memorial* obelisk. To the right is the *Pots and Pans Stone*. Now head 50° NE on path through fence (stone post *"Oldham Way"*) and on over and up moor. Near the top, take the 2nd left path off main path to *Sugarloaf* and on to the inclined *Shaw Rocks*. Keep ahead on path (escape route down in dip) just right of wall. After wall turns 90° left, take right fork to **trig pillar** on **Broadstone Hill**. Now take main path north; as it forks go ahead and pass quarry face on left. Now leave path and go ahead north, off-path, to ruin and down to top of edge at **Ravenstone Brow**. Turn left along edge to fence. Turn left; follow fence uphill for 300m until it turns right. Follow path below fence to gate/stile and on between fine old walls to gate/stile and X-junction. Turn right down **Running Hill Lane**. Take 2nd footpath on right to lane. Turn right and on go right at junction. Follow lane up and down and up to *Diggle Hotel* ahead. Turn left over the railway and left again to the car park at the *Huddersfield Narrow Canal*.

On the path through Sugarloaf to Shaw Rocks ahead (May 24)

The war memorial overlooks the Saddleworth Valley (May 24). The seat does, too!

Far Left. *Not much beer drunk at the Church Inn!* **Above.** *The ruin is a good guide to Ravenstone Brow.* **Left.** *The trig pillar on Broadstone Hill was re-sited by the Saddleworth Fell Runners after it was vandalised in 1998.*

| 03 | **Digley Reservoir, Bilberry Reservoir, Dean Clough and Black Hill** |

Digley Reservoir (Aug 27)

This outing to Black Hill skirts Digley and Bilberry Reservoirs then embarks up the short but wild Dean Clough passing its two waterfalls. The Pennine Way is taken to the trig pillar on Black Hill and we return to the reservoirs by the straight track of Issues Road.

Length 13 kms / 8.13 miles **Map** O/S Explorer OL1, *Dark Peak Area*, West Sheet **Start/Finish** Digley Reservoir north car park at SE 111 071. If full, there is a second car park south of the headwall. Limited bus service from Huddersfield/Glossop/Holmfirth to Holmbridge, Woodhead Road. Take track left (Digley Road) of, or minor road right of *Bridge Tavern* to the car park. Add 2½ kms to the route. Metroline 0113 245 7676. **Terrain** Easy to follow level paths and tracks are followed by an off-path ascent of Dean Clough where care has to be taken and also during the off-path way to Issues Road. Most routes to Black Hill, including ours, have been tamed in recent years by the laying of Yorkshire flagstones. Gone are the knee-deep forays through sloppy peat. Purists moan! **Refreshments** None on route. *The Bridge Tavern* at Holmbridge.
When To Go /What's There As with most Dark Peak walks, this is at its best when the heather is in bloom around the reservoirs and in Dean Clough. There is also bell heather, bilberry and small stands of cross-leaved heath. Larger plants include foxglove and rose bay willowherb. An occasional ring ouzel may be spotted at the old quarries and we once saw a female hen harrier. Buzzard and peregrine falcon are more frequently observed. Other birds include curlew, golden plover, wheatear and waterfowl on the reservoirs. As well as the two fine waterfalls in Dean Clough, a smaller one is passed on the descent to Issues Road. Half a km east of the trig pillar lie the remains of a Fairey Swordfish which came down in January 1940, killing the pilot. You will need a GPS personal navigator and either patience or luck to find the scant wreckage which is quoted as being at SE 08338 04762 (Cunningham, 2006). The search will also add a km and time to the walk.

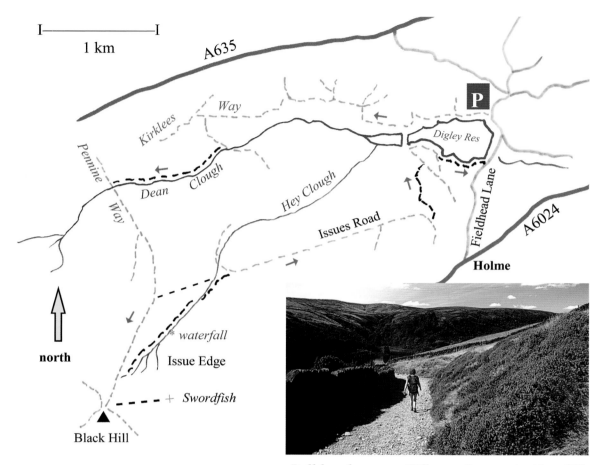

Bell heather near Bilberry Reservoir (Aug 27)

Bilberry Reservoir is just west of Digley Reservoir (Aug 27)

Route Walk to the car park entrance and turn right up the path. After 200m don't go right into old quarry but keep ahead on the main path which runs down to a fork. Go right and soon the path leads down steps and later delivers a fine view (seat). Here, go right at the fork and the path later turns 90° right to meet X-paths. Turn left onto track. After barns stay on track (not ladder stile right) and go through gate and pass a footpath off to the right. Pass dwelling (*Goodbent Lodge*) and 250m on, leave track and go over wall step-stile on left. Follow path left of wall down field. Go over stile and bear left pleasantly down to a footbridge. Here, the left and wider of the two streams on the right leads up ***Dean Clough*** and is best ascended up the right bank. Cross the stones to start up *Dean Clough*. About 400m after the second of two waterfalls (of about 3m in height, photo) and, at a conspicuous isolated and undercut rock on the right, the ***Pennine Way*** crosses the stream. So turn left, cross stream and follow laid path steeply uphill. Soon path is paved with Yorkshire flags from old mills and undulates up the moor. Paving ends then a rocky path and cairns lead the way to more paving and the trig pillar on **Black Hill**. Retrace your steps for about 400m, then at SE 0802 605182, turn right and follow right bank of Issue Clough (50°) steeply down to **Issues Road**. (If you want an easier route, continue down paving for another 500m then, 20m after a small cairn on left, at SE 08238 05760, follow the path on right, 70°, to the track). Once gained, follow track for 1½ kms (gates, stile). After a path joins from the right there's a seat on the left. Soon after, track bends to right. Here, turn sharp left. Follow this track down (gate) until it performs a U-turn to the left. Here, walk ahead down grassy path left of stream and through coppice to stile and on to T-junction. Turn right, go through gate and follow path to south car park. Turn left, cross headwall of ***Digley Reservoir*** then turn left at junction (note spillway shaft) up to north car park.

At the elevated trig pillar on Black Hill (April 24). In spring, skylarks sing above you.

On the track of Issues Road (April 28) **Inset.** *A curlew came-a-calling, too!*

At the upper waterfall in Dean Clough (Aug 10)

Ramsden Reservoir, Ruddle Clough, Hades and Elysium !

Herbage Hill from the path to the old quarries (Aug 16)

The annual Birds of Prey downhill ski race at Beaver Creek, USA is also called the race of Heaven and Hell. This walk is hardly that but we do visit hell (Hades) and heaven (Elysium) after a fine walk through stunning scenery, reached without too much effort.

Length 12 kms / 7.5 miles **Map** O/S Explorer OL1, *Dark Peak Area*, West Sheet
Start/Finish Ramsden Reservoir car park, 2 kms SW of Holmbridge, off the A6024 at SE 115 055. Buses from Holmfirth and Huddersfield stop at the church in Holmbridge. Ask for Woodhead Lane. Metroline 0113 245 7676. This would add 3 kms to the walk.
Terrain The route is easy to follow on a mix of farmland paths and tracks together with woodland tracks and 3 kms of paths up and over moors on access land; tricky in mist.
Refreshments None on route. Pub in Holmbridge; the works in Holmfirth, 3 kms NE.
When To Go/What's There An exhilarating walk for all seasons. In spring the curlews return and their call haunts the high moors. Common sandpiper and oystercatcher visit Snailsden Reservoir, but you're more likely to see Canada geese there. The walk is at its best late summer when the ling and bell heather bloom, the bilberries ripen and the berries of the rowan turn red. The flowers in the woodland glades on the way to Reynard Clough attract speckled wood, small heath, meadow brown, small white, gatekeeper and, if they're over from the near continent, painted lady butterflies. Common hawker dragonflies hunt here, too. Buzzard, kestrel and peregrine hunt larger prey. Other plants include foxglove, burdock ("sticky buds", photo, right), wood sorrel, scented mayweed, tormentil, spearwort, St John's-wort, hard fern and crowberry. We have seen stoats at Hades: but the once immaculate dry-stone-walling of this moribund hamlet's name is sadly sliding into ruin. There is a welcome seat by a stream before Hades.

A conceivably arctic scene at a frozen Snailsden Reservoir (March 7, 2010)

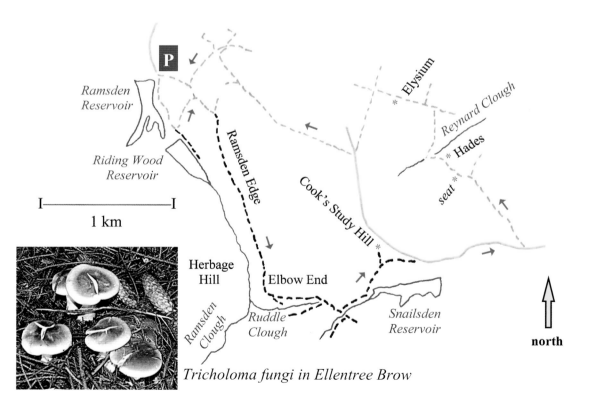

Tricholoma fungi in Ellentree Brow

Route Turn left out of the car park and walk south on the track, above ***Ramsden Reservoir*** on the right. After 400m, turn left up the track opposite a house. Stay on the wide track as it snakes uphill. About 60m after an old cattle grid and gate and, where the track swings 90° left, walk ahead (signed *Access Point*) on the permissive path. Go through gate ahead and continue on the walled path. Soon the way ahead opens to a heathery, old track and passes old quarries on the left. Track ends after last quarry to reach fence ahead. Turn left, uphill, and then right following the fence. Continue ahead on path as fence falls away right. Soon there are views up ***Ramsden Clough*** to the right. Path then rises and forks: take the fainter left path which rounds a shoulder of **Elbow End** (following low posts) then runs up the left bank of ***Ruddle Clough*** to reach a gate in fence at the top of the clough. Through, go right a little and follow main path which runs 116° (eastish) over the moor; beside grouse butts on the left. Path reaches watercourse ahead and footbridge. Don't cross, but turn left to reach ***Snailsden Reservoir***, where the way ahead becomes a track rising to pass **Cook's Study Hill** on left and on to meet road. Turn right. After ½ km turn left over wall stile. Follow track which passes ruins of **Hades** then rounds scenic ***Reynard Clough*** to track junction. Turn left, go over stone stile and pass **Elysium** on left to reach X-tracks. Turn left and walk up to road. Cross and go up track on right which passes heather and pine plantation on left before descending. Here are fine views to Black Hill, West Nab, Digley Reservoir and Holmfirth. When the track turns 90° left go through gate ahead and down walled path. Go through gate and, after 30m, turn left at junction, then soon left again on path beside wall on right down to stile. Over, keep ahead (not left) and follow path downhill. A number of ways soon lead ahead down to the car park.

Passing the heather-clad old quarries **Above.** *Passing hell, too! (both Aug 16)*

Ramsden Reservoir and Holme Moss mast from the lane at the start of the walk (Aug 16)

On the way to Ruddle Clough, with Ramsden Clough ahead (Aug 16)

05

Heyden Brook, Bailie Causeway Moss and Ramsden Clough

Looking down on Yateholme Reservoir from the path back to Holme Moss Car Park
Inset. *Mountain hare in flight across Bailie Causeway Moss (April 26)*

This short, tough but exciting route, wholly on access land, first descends to wild Heyden Brook from Holme Moss, then rises over rough moor to Bailie Causeway Moss. From here, a path leads to the scenic cleft of Ramsden Clough and an optional aircraft wreck.

Length 9 kms / 5.63 miles **Map** O/S Explorer OL1, *Dark Peak Area*, West Sheet
Start/Finish Holme Moss Car Park off the A6024 at SE 097 039. No public transport.
Refreshments Occasional ice cream van in car park
Terrain This walk should be taken slowly as there is much rough ground, not all on paths. Heyden Brook itself has to be crossed a number of times, so trekking poles are recommended for balance. Energy-sapping tussocks have to be crossed for about 500m up to the rim of Dewhill Naze. But, taken steadily, this is fine, wild adventure. Take GPS and also be skilled in map and compass as the weather can change very rapidly up here.
When To Go/What's There The beauty of Ramsden Clough is best appreciated when the heather blooms (see front jacket) but is a delight at any time. In late April and May green hairstreak butterflies emerge in good numbers at Heyden Brook. At that time the boggy patches have marsh violets: later, bog asphodel, marsh pennywort and foxglove flower. There's the odd wren, dipper and wheatear and also hard fern. A number of *Sphagnum* moss flushes support common hawker dragonflies. Liverworts grow where the flushes leach into the brook, over which water crickets glide. Buzzards soar above the moors; mountain hares flee across them and lizards bask on them during summer sun. There are small numbers of curlew, skylark and meadow pipit. Wreckage of the *Consolidated Vultee B-24H-20 Liberator* which crashed in October 1944 at SE 10630 03379 (GPS ref) is an optional visit requiring a 600m detour. A number of memorials are at the site which took the lives of seven crew and two passengers. But one did survive.

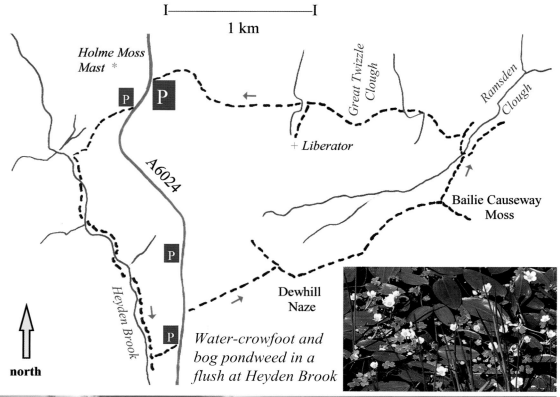

Water-crowfoot and bog pondweed in a flush at Heyden Brook

Passing an eroded bankside in Heyden Brook (April 26)

Route Walk SW on the A6024 for about 300m to meet a lay-by on the west side of the road. Go over stile in lay-by and follow faint path to fence. Keep left of fence and go over stile at fence ahead. Now angle half-left downhill for about 200m to another fence and stile. Over, keep angling down left to pick up path which leads straight down to *Heyden Brook*. Turn left and follow the brook downstream. As you progress, you will have to cross the brook a number of times to avoid boggy patches, steep and eroded bank-sides. After the highest of the eroded banks (photo), the gradient eases on the left bank and an old wall can be seen running down to the left bank. The wall is about 100m after a small fall (photo). Leave the brook after boulder-field on left and pick up a path about 20m right of the wall which runs up to the **A6024** and a lay-by. Turn left uphill on left verge for about 250m then cross road and go over stile. Head uphill on bearing of 70° (right of rocks) over tussocks to rim of **Dewhill Naze** and on to a fence and path. Turn right. Fence changes directions a number of times. At one early turn, path forks, but continue on path by fence. After another km, path leads through peaty areas. Soon after, path leads to a wooden tension post at 90° to fence (the only one you meet). 50m later, the fence is rolled down to allow access to other side (GPS ref SE 11560 03006). Once over, head on bearing of 38° (or if clear head for mast on Emley Moor) for about 400m (crossing 4x4 track) to pick up the path which rounds the head of *Ramsden Clough*. As you follow the left bank the path forks. Go left and uphill a little to see Holme Moss TV Mast ahead. The path runs over the moor; passes a building ruin on the right; rounds horseshoe-shaped *Great Twizzle Clough* and then runs to left of old wall. Soon a distinct watercourse crosses the path at SE 10638 03677. Here, if you want to visit the *Liberator* crash site turn left up the watercourse for about 300m to the wreckage (perhaps a GPS would help) and then return to the path. Follow path in the direction of the mast for about another km and finally two gates in fences allow access to the car park.

The small fall in Heyden Brook (April 26). The wall to find the exit path from the clough is about 100m downstream.

On the path above Ramsden Clough (Aug 23). See also front jacket.

Reading one of the memorial plaques at the crash site of the Liberator (Aug 23, 2008)

06

Lad's Leap, Hollins Clough, Chew Reservoir and Laddow Rocks

Off to the hills on The Pennine Way at the start of the walk (April 23)

This tough adventure for those with map and compass skills starts at Crowden and rises steeply to the falls at Lad's Leap; off-path follows gentle Hollins Clough to an isolated trig pillar before falling to Chew Reservoir, the highest in England. An optional extension to an aircraft wreck is followed by a trek back over Laddow Moss to the Pennine Way.

Length 11 kms / 6.88 miles **Map** O/S Explorer OL1, *Dark Peak Area*, West Sheet
Start/Finish Crowden car park off the A628 at SK 072 993. National Express route 350.
Terrain Easy to follow tracks and paths with 3 kms of off-path moor up Hollins Clough and down to Chew Reservoir. A visit to the *Tiger Moth* wreck will add 1½ kms to the route. The path down from Laddow Rocks on the *Pennine Way* is rocky and arduous.
Refreshments In summer, the campsite shop near the car park and conveniences is open.
When To Go/What's There The few remnants of the *Tiger Moth DH82A* biplane which crashed in April 1945 killing the pilot lie SW of the headwall of Chew Reservoir at SE 03353 01584 (GPS acc 4m). A round wooden stake is beside the remains. In November, the shards are speckled with poppies; a reminder that such sites are visited by relatives and that trophy hunters should lay-off. We have trekked up to Chew Reservoir on many occasions but it seems devoid of water-birds: I guess they prefer the warmer climes of Dovestone Reservoir 280 metres below! However, other wildlife is hardier: a pool near the trig pillar supports frogs, whirlygig beetles, common hawker and black darter dragonflies. Pond skaters, water crickets, water beetles and stonefly larvae can be seen in the clear waters of the stream bubbling down Hollins Clough. Harder to spot, unless flushed, are the mountain hare, snipe and golden plover. Curlew and skylark sing in early summer. Lower down, at the start of the walk, pied and grey wagtail and dipper may be spotted by the water and woodpeckers and squirrel in the trees. Small heath and green-veined white are frequent butterflies. In June, cottongrasses line the path to Lad's Leap.

The banks of peat in upper Hollins Clough (April 23)

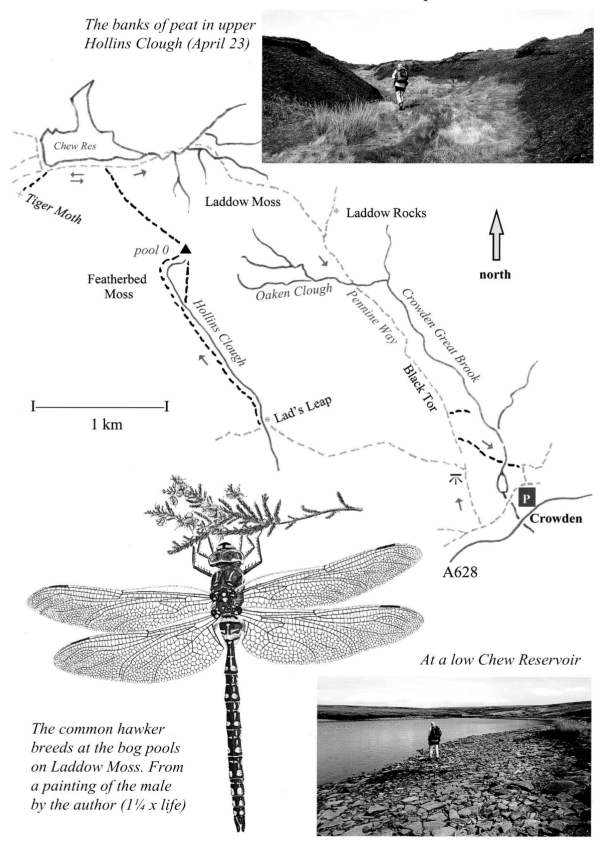

Chew Res

Tiger Moth

Laddow Moss

Laddow Rocks

north

pool 0

Featherbed Moss

Oaken Clough

Hollins Clough

Pennine Way

Crowden Great Brook

Black Tor

I———————————I
1 km

* Lad's Leap

P

Crowden

A628

The common hawker breeds at the bog pools on Laddow Moss. From a painting of the male by the author (1¼ x life)

At a low Chew Reservoir

Route From the car park go to the conveniences, pass the campsite on the left and turn left at the X-tracks ahead. After a gate, follow the metalled track uphill and, just before a pine wood on the left, turn right onto the **Pennine Way**. The way leads up over stiles and a stone footbridge (with benchmark and TC 1912 carving); through another gate/stile (another benchmark on boulder after) and on through a gate into access land (there's a memorial cairn by the wood). Here, turn left off the *Pennine Way* and follow path uphill. As it forks, take right path which climbs to meet an old wall on the left. Turn 90° left here and this path rises and runs right of a wall to a stile and becomes steeper before easing. Follow the path across the moor (some cairns) to the deep cleft of **Lad's Leap**. Descend to and cross the stream then head off right on a bearing of 342°, soon to pick up a faint path on the left bank of a stream. The path becomes more pronounced as you head up the watercourse, which is **Hollins Clough**. After about 1½ kms, a path leaves the watercourse on the right near the top of the moor and rises up the crest of an eroded peat grough. Faint paths lead ahead before swinging right to the **trig pillar**. Alternatively, you could stay in the watercourse which, too, eventually swings right to reveal the pillar ahead, at SE 046 011. Now set compass to 322° and follow dry watercourses and faint trails down the moor to **Chew Reservoir**. (To find **Tiger Moth** remains, turn left on waterside path to headwall. Set compass to 230° and walk SW for about 300m; then use GPS. There is a wooden stake at the scant remains). Our walk turns right at the reservoir and follows the well-used path as it rises up **Laddow Moss** passing cairns to a stile at the top of the moor. Over, the path now descends to the *Pennine Way* again, just south of **Laddow Rocks** (viewpoint). Turn right and carefully descend the rocky and steep path. It crosses the stream at the head of **Oaken Clough** and continues to fall for about another 1½ kms. Above to the right is **Black Tor** and, opposite the end of the edge, a grassy path leaves the *Pennine Way* on the left (about 200m before trees ahead); becomes more worn and leads down to a post. Bear left to stile and footbridge over weir and **Crowden Brook**. Go through gate ahead and bear right down track to T-junction. Turn left to meet gate; cross track ahead to car park.

Frogspawn-spotting at the pool, with other walkers bagging the trig pillar (April 23)

When the falls at Lad's Leap are dry there are some easy scrambles (June 16)

At the pitiful remains of the Tiger Moth (as of Dec 5, 2009). If you're going to the site, note the aspect of Chew Reservoir from here and the grough running from right to left.

Passing Lower Swineshaw Reservoir en route to Hollingworthall Moor above (Aug 8)

The moors and reservoirs just to the east of Greater Manchester are seldom visited by walkers from elsewhere. However, if you're in the area or want a change from the popular haunts, then this route to the high moors is a fine introduction to this outpost.

Length 11 kms / 6.88 miles **Map** O/S Explorer OL1, *Dark Peak Area*, West Sheet
Start/Finish Besom Lane car park in Stalybridge Country Park at Millbrook at SJ 978 994. Besom Lane is off the B6175 to the left of the old *Commercial Inn*. There is a further car park for the Country Park at Oakwell, to the left of the *Royal Oak*, SW of Besom Lane. Bus numbers 218, 343 and 348 run every few minutes from the Stalybridge and Mossley areas to Millbrook. Ask for Huddersfield Road Parkway.
Refreshments None on route. Pubs and shops near to car park.
Terrain Most of the height is gained on a gently rising metalled track which leads to paths over rough pasture and then heather moor. There is a steep descent from the top.
When To Go/What's There A fine outing whatever the season, but in late summer the heather blooms and there are wonderful grasses on the descent from the moor. Bird-life on the water is dominated by Canada geese, but in the sky we have seen kestrel and peregrine falcon. As you rise up Hollingworthall Moor, a majestic panorama of The Peak is revealed including Dovestone Rocks at Greenfield, the duo of South Head and Mount Famine, Kinder Scout and, with binoculars, the cone of Shutlingsloe and Jodrell Bank radio telescope on the Cheshire Plain. Also with bins, you can watch planes land at Manchester Airport on a bearing of 240° from the trig pillar. Flowers include rose bay willowherb, devil's-bit scabious, mugwort, stinking chamomile, fodder vetch, knapweed, Himalayan balsam, hawkweeds, wood sage, tormentil, cotton-grass and burdock. These attract butterflies including wall, comma, meadow brown, gatekeeper and peacock.

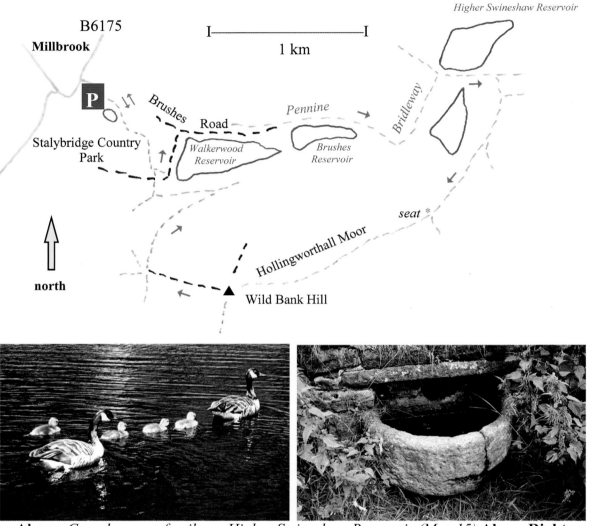

Above. *Canada goose family on Higher Swineshaw Reservoir (May 15)* **Above Right.** *Ancient well beside Brushes Road* **Below Right.** *At the trig pillar on Wild Bank Hill*

Left. *Lake in Stalybridge CP*

Route Go through the opening in the car park, left of the information board and signed to *Walkerwood Reservoir*. Follow path left of lake and bear left over a footbridge. Bear right at path junction; cross boarding and go up steps. Turn left at a path junction and left again at another and keep ahead to a lane. Turn left and cross the headwall of **Walkerwood Reservoir**. Turn right and follow the lane to gates. Keep ahead on what is now part of the **Pennine Bridleway** and signed to *Tintwistle*. Pass an old quarry on the left and continue on the metalled lane which soon reaches **Higher Swineshaw Reservoir**. Turn right; cross the headwall and go through metal gate. Keep ahead at junction, heading towards a pylon (fingerpost signed *public footpath*). Go under the overhead cables to gate/stile and on up the path to a junction. Turn right, fingerpost signed *footpath*. Path rises above Lower Swineshaw Reservoir and at a fingerpost keep right on the worn path to a "gate" in a wall. Cross the field ahead to gap in wall. Through, bear left, uphill, to ladder stile and seat. Don't go over the stile but turn right and follow wall on left (path not obvious) to a wall ahead and a step stile about 40m right of wall corner. Over, bear left, uphill. Path levels out to reach a stile in fence then rises again up **Hollingworthall Moor** to another stile in fence and on up the moor to the **trig pillar**. From here, walk ahead (west) down path left of wall ruin. Path becomes quite steep. Just after the heather ends at a wall junction, turn right. Path follows south bank of Walkerwood Reservoir then swings left towards the headwall. Keep ahead at path junction to reach another junction at posts and heather hillock where main path swings left. Here, turn right and go over stile in fence. Path runs down to stile in wall ahead and a lane. Turn left on lane then immediately right through metal barrier to path in **Stalybridge Country Park** again. Turn left; bear right at junction and right again at another. Go down steps; over boarding; keep left at junction and on to car park.

Through the wonderful grassland near the end of the walk (Aug 8)

Top Left. *Painted lady butterfly beside Higher Swineshaw Reservoir.*

Top Right. *Harridge Pike from Walkerwood Reservoir.*

Left. *Higher Swineshaw Reservoir (all Aug 8).*

Walkerwood Reservoir and Harridge Pike viewed on the descent from the trig pillar on Hollingworthall Moor. The lake in Stalybridge CP is left of the reservoir (Aug 8).

08 | Dowstone Rocks, Birchen Bank Moss and Near Black Clough (Bleaklow)

Woodhead Bridge and Reservoir from the top of the ascent track (Aug 11)

This excursion to north Bleaklow easily gains height before a steep pull gains the views of Woodhead Reservoir from the buttresses of Deer Knoll and Dowstone Rocks. Hard work off-path leads to an aircraft wreck and a descent to the beauty of Birchen Bank Clough.

Length 11 kms / 6.88 miles **Map** O/S Explorer OL1, *Dark Peak Area*, West Sheet
Start/Finish Parking for about 10 cars just off the B6105 as it turns 90° to join the A628 at SK 081 993 and where the *Longdendale Trail* meets the road. At the weekends the places soon fill up so start early, otherwise parking at Torside will add 4 kms to the walk.
Refreshments None on route so stock the rucksack.
Terrain A mixture of low-level tracks; narrow, high moorland paths; off-path moor and peat groughs to negotiate and, should you wish to visit the upper waterfalls in Near Black Clough, then there is a short but very steep and pathless bank of vegetation to descend and ascend back to the path. It would be dangerous to try and reach the lower race of the fall. Map and compass skills needed if misty; GPS and binoculars to find the Wellington.
When To Go/What's There As part of the route lies on grouse-shooting moors it would be best to go before August 12th - but as near as you can to that date so as to enjoy the heather in flower, too! We visit the crash site of a Wellington R1011 bomber which came down on Birchen Bank Moss on 30th January 1943, killing three of the five crew. The GPS reference is SK 10545 98576 (acc. 4m). A little lower, cloudberry flourishes and mountain hares flee. Lower still, beside the *Longdendale Trail*, flowers include great and rose bay willowherb, knapweed, harebell, foxglove, trefoils, vetches and hawkweeds. The marshy areas and drains support marsh orchids, pond skaters, whirlygig beetles and emerald damselfly, black darter and common hawker dragonflies. Butterflies include small heath, small skipper, green-veined white, meadow brown and gatekeeper.

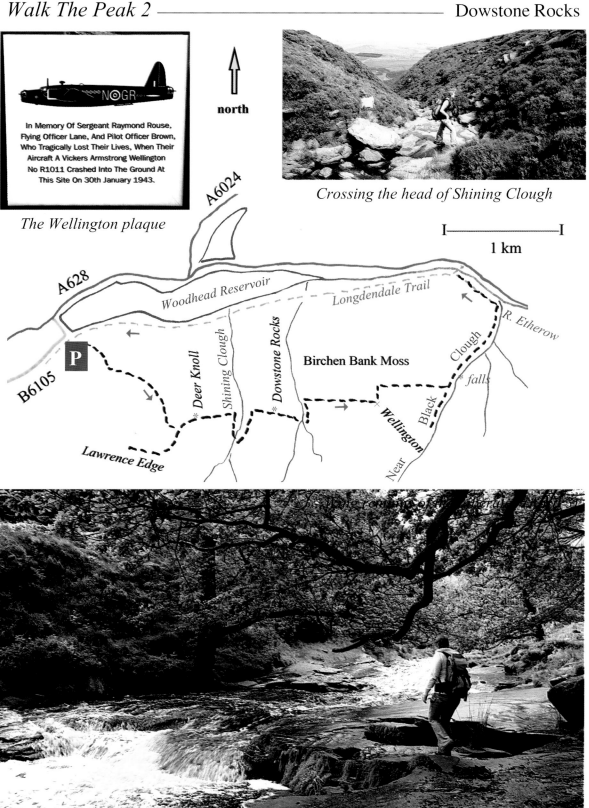

In Memory Of Sergeant Raymond Rouse,
Flying Officer Lane, And Pilot Officer Brown,
Who Tragically Lost Their Lives, When Their
Aircraft A Vickers Armstrong Wellington
No R1011 Crashed Into The Ground At
This Site On 30th January 1943.

The Wellington plaque

north

Crossing the head of Shining Clough

I————————I
1 km

A6024

A628

Woodhead Reservoir

Longdendale Trail

R. Etherow

P

B6105

Deer Knoll

Shining Clough

Dowstone Rocks

Birchen Bank Moss

Black Clough

falls

Wellington

Near

Lawrence Edge

Arriving at the bottom of beautiful Birchen Bank Clough (Aug 11)

Route Inside the car parking area, cross the **Longdendale Trail** and go through the gate - which may have had the *Access Land* plate removed - and walk to the pylon. Opposite, a distinct track can be seen leading uphill. Follow this all the way up until it terminates at a small area of level ground, used for parking 4x4s. From here, the way ahead is off-path so walk on up, bearing left until the "summit edge" can be seen as amphitheatre-shaped. To the right are the rocks of **Lawrence Edge** but left a grassy/heather shoulder can be seen. Ascend this to the "edge", which is indiscernible at this point. Don't head up the terrain, but turn left and look for a narrow path which runs along the edge. Continue on even if you don't find the path until the flat rocks of **Deer Knoll** are reached. Pick up the path here which soon veers right to cross the brook at the head of the deep cleft of **Shining Clough**. Next, the impressive buttresses of **Dowstone Rocks** appear, their true height revealed with a retrospective glance. Another detour right is made to breach another unnamed clough. Here there is fencing and a stile to access fording of the brook. Now turn left and follow a path down to grouse butts. At No 5 (the second down) set compass to 94° east and walk ½ km over **Birchen Bank Moss** to the site of the **Wellington** crash. From here, walk about 100 m down the moor then turn right (east) across the moor to reach the path running above **Near Black Clough** after another ½ km. Turn left; soon the waterfalls appear below (optional, very steep descent). Near the end of the path it swings sharp right down to Birchen Bank Clough. Turn left, follow track downstream. It veers left above the **River Etherow**, which is crossed via a bridge. Turn left to the Longdendale Trail, passing the three tunnel entrances and platforms. Take the left path back to the car parking area.

At the upper falls in Near Black Clough. It is not safe to descend to the lower race.

On the buttresses of Dowstone Rocks (Aug 11)

Reading the memorial plaque at the scant remains of the Wellington (Aug 11, 2008)

09

Lightside, Dog Rock, Harrop Moss and Cock Hill

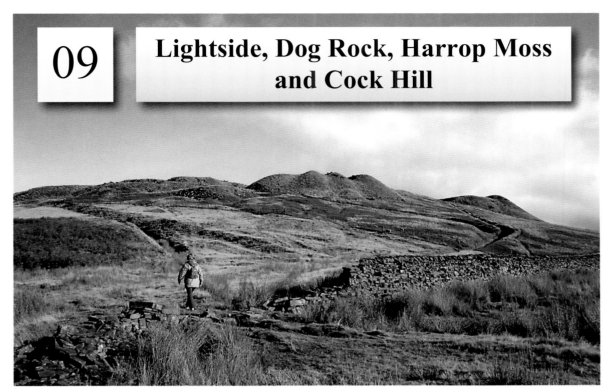

At the bottom of the old quarries beneath Cock Hill (Oct 16)

This short but fairly tough trip gains all the height at the start of the walk up the shoulder of Lightside, which itself rises above the ancient path of Doctor's Gate. The way then leads to Dog Rock and a viewpoint above the spectacular clough down which tumbles Yellowslacks Brook. Paths over Harrop Moss lead to a trig pillar and a rustic descent.

Length 9 kms / 5.63 miles **Map** O/S Explorer OL1, *Dark Peak Area*, West Sheet
Start/Finish Cars can be parked beside the Old Glossop bus terminus at SK 045 949. Trains/buses run from the Manchester area to Glossop and service 390 to the terminus.
Refreshments None on the route. Glossop has just about every possibility.
Terrain Although 80% of the route is over access land, there are paths throughout the walk. However, the route described should be carefully followed as the path alternatives are many. Compass bearings are quoted so you will need to follow a given bearing (see p.16). The trek across Harrop Moss and on to the shooting cabin crosses many peaty watercourses, so go after dry periods or when the ground is frozen. Footbridges and treaded boards laid by the grouse fraternity fortunately avoid the wettest bits. There are very steep drops from atop Dog Rock and care is even needed on the walled path down.
When To Go/What's There As previously mentioned, go when the ground is hard. A walk for all seasons but route-finding tricky after snow. Take your time on the ascent and enjoy the expanding views behind, too. Birds in season include curlew, skylark, golden plover, raven and short-eared owl. On Harrop Moss, mountain hares are many. Belted Galloway, pied wagtail, broom, foxgloves and yellow flag are seen on the walk in. We once saw six of the unique vapourer moth larvae on these walls (photo, right).

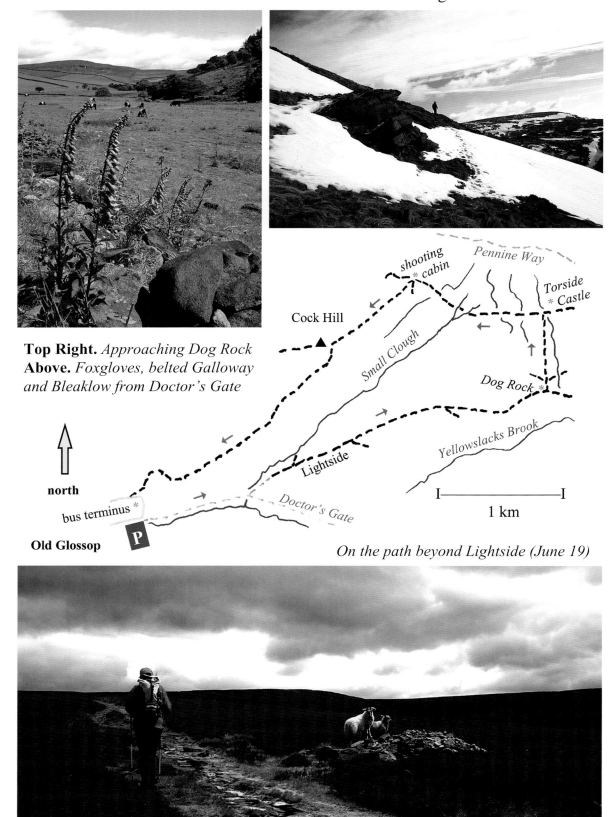

Top Right. *Approaching Dog Rock*
Above. *Foxgloves, belted Galloway
and Bleaklow from Doctor's Gate*

shooting
* cabin

Pennine Way

Cock Hill

Torside
* Castle

Small Clough

Dog Rock *

north

Lightside

Yellowslacks Brook

bus terminus *

Doctor's Gate

1 km

Old Glossop P

On the path beyond Lightside (June 19)

Route From the bus terminus take the signed footpath which runs west and is the start of ***Doctor's Gate***. After ¾ km a gate ahead is reached. Ignore this and turn left up the steps and go through another gate. Head up the path and go through the gate into access land. Head up path and at a broken wall keep ahead (not narrow path left). To the left are now views of the ***old quarries*** on the descent route and the trig pillar on **Cock Hill** right of the hummocks. Head up the shoulder of **Lightside** to stile in fence. Over, follow path up through the heather to another stile in fence. Over, keep ahead on path which runs just below the hill-top and past rocks to a fence. Here, don't descend to the right but follow the path by the fence-posts uphill. Path later runs between the posts and leads to the crags high above the chasm containing ***Yellowslacks Brook***. The highest crag (and the next to the last) is ***Dog Rock*** and a fine viewpoint. From here, head 20° north for about 50m to stile in fence. Over, take the middle path (ahead) which runs north. Follow the watercourse, posts and grouse butts downhill (if ground is wet use left bank of watercourse) until a footbridge with stepped boarding in the watercourse is reached. (About 100m half-right, the low mound of ***Torside Castle*** can be seen). Turn left up the boarding and follow the path west, crossing a number of watercourses by footbridges and boards to reach a small ***shooting cabin*** (currently being renovated) after about 1 km. Now turn left but leave the track on the path which runs 220° south. After 100m, at an old stone grouse butt, bear right at the fork on bearing of 250° to reach the **trig pillar** on Cock Hill after ¾ km. You can only see the pillar when about 50m from it. Now take the path left (200°) down to the old quarries. Keep ahead on main path through the quarries to meet another path. Ahead, path runs down to a gate at a meeting of a fence and wall. Through, follow wall on left then turn left on to path between walls. Follow path; pass through three gates on the way, all way down to join a lane (Charles Lane). Lane soon joins a housing road. Turn sharp left and follow road up, round and down to the **Old Glossop Bus Terminus** and the start of the walk.

Mountain hare tracks at the footbridge (!) opposite Torside Castle (Feb 11)

On the way up Lightside, with the old quarries descent route above the walker (Feb 11)

Looking back from atop Dog Rock (June 19)

10

Etherow Country Park, Hackingknife and Botham's Hall

Though the lovely meadows on the way to Hackingknife (July 25)

A walk full of variety and interest starting from Etherow Country Park and rising to a dichotomous view from Hackingknife, where Greater Manchester conurbations contrast with the vast (and precious) wilderness of Bleaklow and Kinder Scout plateaux.

Length 13 kms / 8.13 miles **Map** O/S Explorer OL1, *Dark Peak Area*, West Sheet
Start/Finish Etherow Country Park car park just off the B6104 at SJ 965 909 (P&D)
Bus service 394 runs between Glossop/Marple/Hazel Grove. Service Nos 383 and 384
run from Stockport to Compstall via Marple railway station. Traveline 0871 200 2233
Refreshments Café next to Visitor Centre; *Rock Tavern* on A626 back to Country Park
Terrain Easy to follow paths and tracks. A few short sections of bridleways are stony
and dark. There is a 1 km main road stretch on a safe footpath - and here is the pub!
When To Go/What's There The Country Park is popular and busy most weekends due
to the easy, level paths around the lakes. Once you rise out of the park you will probably
be alone until you reach the war memorial and toposcope on Hackingknife. As well as
the usual wildfowl, the lakes have little and great crested grebe, tufted duck, cormorant
and the striking mandarin duck. The park has good habitats for butterflies: one tree-top
dwelling species, purple hairstreak, occasionally is seen feeding on bramble (blackberry)
flowers. Down at Keg pool, a fine wood sculpture of a kingfisher overlooks the pool. It
was donated by Frank and Marion Grisbrook. As well as the bird-life, brown hawker
and common darter dragonflies and common blue and large red damselflies flutter over
the water in summer. Beside the pool yellow flag, greater reedmace, yellow and purple
loosestrife are found. Amphibious bistort floats on the water. Himalayan balsam girdles
many woodland paths and will soon dominate the native flora. The meadows support
harebell, yellow rattle, betony, greater bird's-foot trefoil, yarrow, fodder vetch, meadow
vetchling and mallow. These attract many butterflies. Skylarks sing above the fields.

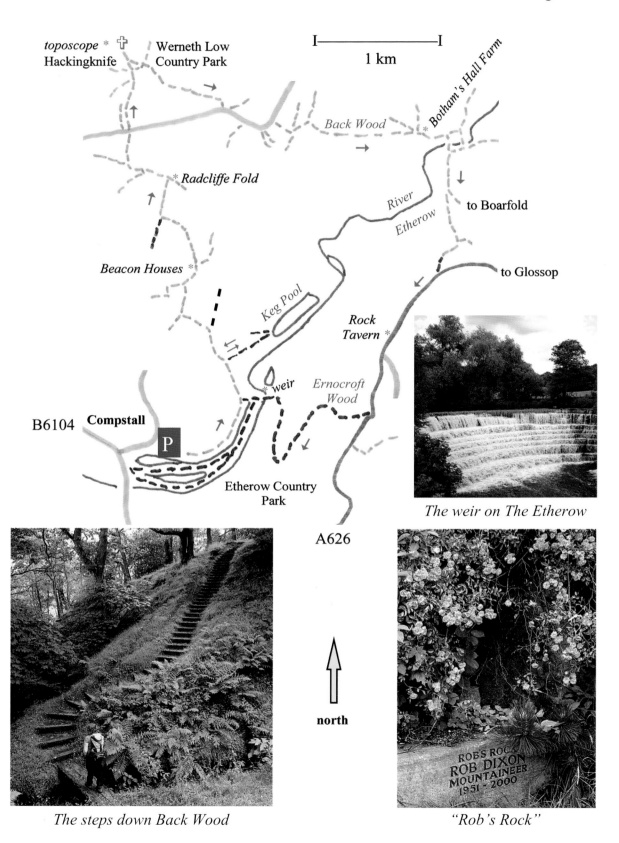

toposcope * ✝   Werneth Low
Hackingknife   Country Park

1 km

Botham's Hall Farm

Back Wood

* *Botham's Hall Farm*

* *Radcliffe Fold*

River Etherow

to Boarfold

Beacon Houses *

to Glossop

Keg Pool

Rock Tavern *

* weir

Ernocroft Wood

B6104   **Compstall**

P

Etherow Country Park

The weir on The Etherow

A626

north

The steps down Back Wood

"Rob's Rock"

ROB'S ROCK
ROB DIXON
MOUNTAINEER
1951 - 2000

Route Pass the Visitor Centre on path left of lake; keep ahead on track ignoring two f/bs on right then turn left (signed *Keg Wood/Sunny Corner*). Pass PCs on left and bear right on track that rises through woodland to a signed post. To see **Keg Pool** turn right, but return by same path to post. Onwards, follow *Valley Way* to seat and rubbing plaque. 100m on, turn left (waymark post) and follow path up and then beside wood to gates/stiles. After 1st stile turn right up field to stile and metalled track. Turn right up track. After 150m, at right bend, leave track at gate at **Beacon Houses**. Go up field to stile and on to another and yet again to a stile and gate on the left. Over, pass circular fold on right (seat, but nettles) to narrow bridleway. Turn right to junction at **Radcliffe Fold**. Turn left, pass houses and track bears right up to a road. Cross. Take the right path which runs beside Werneth Low Golf Course, passes Tee 10 and then runs down to a gate and ahead to the War Memorial and **toposcope** on **Hackingknife** in Werneth Low Country Park. From the memorial, retrace your steps for about 30m then bear left at waymarked post and on to cross track via gates. Follow path to road. Go ahead down road until, after left bend, turn right (signed *Back Wood*). Follow the narrow, shaded path down to track. Cross, follow stony path down to track. Turn right, keep ahead and the way opens out to field and gate. 30m on, and left of large oak, leave track and go over stile into **Back Wood**. Follow path through edge of wood to stile and ahead down a spiral of steps to cross stream and join grassy path. Bear right, go through gate then turn right (signed *Hodgefold*). Here, on left, just before **Botham's Hall Farm** is memorial stone to Rob Dixon. Follow track for about 250m, then go over the 2nd footbridge on right and ahead to gate (or right to river, photo below). Bear right between fences to gate. Through, turn left. As fence bends left, leave it and walk ahead south (towards hill) across field to stile. Over, bear right to stile. Don't go over but turn left (waymark post). After 50m, turn sharp right (post but no arrow this direction) up to stile (waymark). Cross stream and go up to stile. Over, follow path into field and on up past old gatepost to right of gate and track. Go ahead, bear right and follow track ahead to the **A626**. Turn right and use the pavement to the **Rock Tavern**. About 700m after, turn right into **Etherow CP** (signed). Follow path down wood, always staying on the main path (signs to *Country Park* and later *Car Park*) to the **weir**. Cross bridge over River Etherow; turn left down steps; cross f/b over canal overflow and, ahead, you can either stay beside left bank of lake or cross f/b and go left between lake and canal back to car park.

A fine picnic site beside the River Etherow (July 25)

Looking down on Oldham from the toposcope on Hackingknife (July 25)

Bird-watching at Keg Pool from the kingfisher sculpture (July 25)

11 Rowarth, Lantern Pike and Matley Moor

At the toposcope on the summit of Lantern Pike (Aug 25)

Starting from the pretty hamlet of Rowarth, this fairly easy outing passes the historic Little Mill Inn before a stretch of rustic farmland leads to Aspenshaw Hall and easier going. Lantern Pike is breached by a short sharp pull for views of many old friends from a different aspect. The route is then a leisurely stroll up to Knarrs and a descent to a ford.

Length 11 kms / 6.88 miles **Map** O/S Explorer OL1, *Dark Peak Area*, West Sheet
Start/Finish Car park in the hamlet of Rowarth, 4 kms south of Charlesworth and 3½ kms north of New Mills at SK 011 891. No public transport. From Charlesworth the lanes are very narrow. The roads from New Mills and Marple Bridge are wider and safer.
Terrain There are some awkward stiles and potentially muddy paths to negotiate at the start of the walk, but then the way is on paths, tracks and lanes that are easy to follow.
Refreshments The *Little Mill Inn* at the start or end of the walk (01663 743178)
When To Go/What's There In spring the wheatears and curlews reappear followed by the song of the skylark. Late summer sees the heather flower and the bilberries ripen on the flanks of Lantern Pike. The summit toposcope points to the landmarks and from the path through Wethercotes *The Cage* folly in Lyme Park (Walk 14) is seen to the west. The *Little Mill Inn* has a terrace overlooking the restored but working mill wheel. The original wheel and wheelhouse were swept away in a huge flood in 1930. There has been a mill on the site since 1605. The current building dates from 1781 and was a candlewick mill. The pub currently doubles as a post office and, for those seeking a different type of guest accommodation, there is a Brighton Belle Pullman railway coach to try. Flowers seen throughout the season include fox and cubs, harebell, monkeyflower, wood sorrel, scented mayweed, bell heather, lungwort, foxglove, tormentil and, on the approach to Matleymoor Farm, Michaelmas daisy. Butterflies include wall, comma, small heath, small skipper, meadow brown and green-veined white. Buzzard and kestrel hunt above.

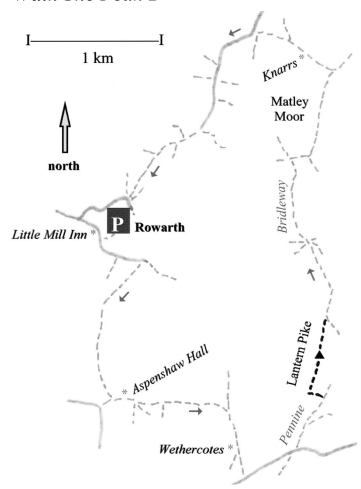

Above. *On the eastern flank of Matley Moor.* **Below.** *Harebells on Matley Moor (Aug 25)*

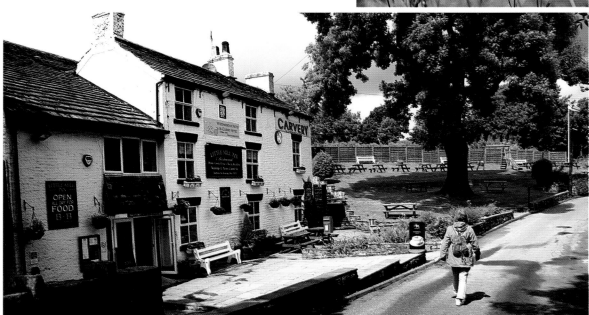

Passing (or about to enter) the Little Mill Inn (July 9)

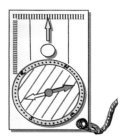

Route Turn left out of the car park. Walk down lane to T-junction and turn left. Pass **Little Mill Inn** on right. After about 150m also pass a fingerpost on the right and walk on another 100m or so to a second post on the right. Here, go over the wall (hardly a stile) and keep left of wall ahead to a wall step-stile. Cross field to metal "ladder-stile" 20m right of gate. Ahead, go through gate and over step-stile left of barn. Cross farmyard to awkward wall step-stile ahead. Round building and follow path across sloping field and left of wall to a wall step-stile. Follow path ahead through bottom of wood to another step-stile and on to lane. Turn left. Pass **Aspenshaw Hall** on left. Keep ahead as lane becomes path. Go through gate and up to T-junction. Turn right. Pass between buildings at **Wethercotes** and on down to lane. Turn left and descend to row of cottages on left. Turn left after last cottage (*5 Windy Knoll*) up the **Pennine Bridleway**. Higher up lane becomes a stony path to gate and *National Trust* sign. Turn left immediately through gate on narrow path steeply uphill. Near the top path swings right and runs up to toposcope on summit of **Lantern Pike**. Follow path ahead and down to rejoin main path. Go through gate and ahead bear left down rutted path to a six-way junction. Go through gate on right and bear left down track and up to junction. Turn right. Pass *Matley Moor Farm* on left and after 100m turn left off track up grassy path to gate/stile. Over, keep left of wall up **Matley Moor** to stile/gate and ahead to track. Turn left. On, go right of house (**Knarrs**) and over wall stile. Bear left down to wall stile. Over, keep just right of wall down to stile then through gate to lane. Turn left down to bottom of hill, where way ahead is through gate or over stile. Follow path to ford which can be turned on right over natural clapper bridge. Over ford, keep ahead up the trail to gate and on to a lane. Turn left down to the hamlet of **Rowarth** and the car park ahead.

On the steep path to the summit ridge of Lantern Pike (Aug 25)

Approaching Blackshaw Farm en route to Matley Moor (Oct 1)

On the descent from Lantern Pike (Aug 25)

12 Barber Booth (Edale), Chapel Gate, Brown Knoll and Jacob's Ladder

Approaching the trig pillar on Brown Knoll (April 15)

This fine circuit of the upper Edale Valley gains the height steadily up the eroded track of Cut Gate before launching out across the moor to Brown Knoll. Here, it is possible to view an aircraft wreck before descending to the head of Jacob's Ladder for another short detour to ancient Edale Cross. Taken leisurely, this is an outing amidst dramatic scenery.

Length 11 kms / 6.88 miles **Map** O/S Explorer OL1, *Dark Peak Area*, West Sheet
Start/Finish Lay-by on the lane from Barber Booth to Upper Booth at SK 107 847. Trains run to Edale from Sheffield/Manchester. This would add 4 kms to the walk.
Terrain Easy to follow paths and tracks over rough terrain. However, the 2½ kms trek over the moor to Brown Knoll could be tricky in fog and, after rain, the moor is soggy to say the least! The descent of Jacob's Ladder is steep and stony so carefully does it!
Refreshments Back in Edale itself are *The Jolly Rambler*, *The Nag's Head* and a café.
When To Go/What's There For a first visit go after a week of dry weather so the stretch of moor to the trig pillar isn't soul-destroying! In early summer, curlew, golden plover and skylarks call. There are a few mountain hares and common lizards. Cross-leaved heath, ling heather and cottongrass bloom in small stands. Foxgloves girdle walls in the valley. As you pass through Lee Farm on the return leg enter the Information Shelter to see the wildlife plaque, information boards and leaflets. There is a donation box, too. Just outside is a stone seat carved on the edge with destinations *Jacob's Ladder*, *Edale Cross* and *Kinder Downfall*. Near to the trig pillar on Brown Knoll lies wreckage of the *Oxford HN594* which crashed in 1945. This event was fully described and photographed in *Walk The Peak* (Walk 12) but is reprised here for those unfamiliar with the area.   *Edale Cross*

Looking back to the Noe Stool on Kinder Scout after descending Jacob's Ladder (Aug 2)

north

Edale Cross

Jacob's Ladder

* falls

I─────────I
1 km

* Lee Farm

Upper Booth

* arched footbridge

to Edale Stn

Brown Knoll ▲

Horsehill Tor

Barber Booth

P →

Peeping through the trees towards Lose Hill (Dec 23)

Cowburn Tunnel

Chapel   Gate

Right. *Lose Hill and Back Tor from Upper Booth (Dec 23)*

Route Turn right out of the lay-by and walk down to the viaduct, where an arched footbridge is on the left (frontispiece photo). Continue down the lane for another 100m then turn right over stile. Follow path right of watercourse to gate and on to stile across from farm track. Now angle left over field to stile. Over, bear left to stile. Over, follow fence to gate. Through, head up to standing stone; keep left of it up to another stone with small seat and on over quite a high stile. Go over another stile ahead and on up to join the eroded track of *Chapel Gate*. Turn right; negotiate gate or stile and head up to a footpath sign (No 98) on the right. Head up past the sign. At the top continue to where the track turns 90° left. Here, turn right on the path (post) across the moor. In view to the left are Combs Edge, Eccles Pike, Chinley Churn and South Head. Follow the path which initially heads 330° north and after 2kms runs 300° to the trig pillar on **Brown Knoll**. If you want to see the *Oxford* remains, head down the moor for one minute on bearing of 296° then return. From the pillar head 360° north over a peat expanse to meet two old walls. Continue north following the path right of the wall and fence then go over one of the access stiles and follow the path down left of the fence and old wall. It turns 90° left and later becomes paved to meet X-paths. To see *Edale Cross*, turn left and follow path over the rise ahead and the medieval cross is on the right. If not, turn right through the gate and go down the path which joins *Jacob's Ladder*. Up to the left, Edale Rocks, The Noe Stool and Woolpacks dominate the Kinder skyline. The stony path becomes a laid staircase. At a cairn, keep left of it on path which falls to cross the fledgeling River Noe by a bridge. Go through the gate and contend with two sets of gates/stiles to reach *Lee Farm* with its Information Shelter on the right. From here the way ahead leads to **Upper Booth** and then on a metalled track back to the lay-by.

Homeward-bound towards Upper Booth at the end of the day (Dec 23)

Leaving Chapel Gate on the path to Brown Knoll, with Cowburn Tunnel air shaft left.

Looking over to Horsehill Tor on a magical winter morning (Dec 23)

13 The Restored Buxworth Canal Basin and Chinley Churn

Heading to Chinley Churn's old quarries with South Head and Mount Famine in view.

This girdle traverse of Chinley Churn delivers fine views from every aspect. It starts from the historically important Buxworth Canal Basin; rises with a steady 300 metre gain in height to Chinley Churn's old quarries before falling to a stroll on a relict "tramway".

Length 10 kms / 6.25 miles **Map** O/S Explorer OL1, *Dark Peak Area*, West Sheet
Start/Finish Car park beside the *Navigation Inn* and Buxworth Canal Basin signposted off the A6 at SK 022 820. Chinley rail station is but 300m from Leaden Knowl where the route could start. Chinley is served by buses: 0870 608 2608; trains: 08457 48 49 50
Terrain A thousand feet of height is gently gained at the start of the walk. Bridleways and paths, particularly on the west flank of Chinley Churn can be waterlogged after prolonged rainfall, but can be out-manoeuvred. Route straightforward; some roadwork.
Refreshments *Navigation Inn* at start/end of walk. Nearby Chinley has cafés, chips etc.
When To Go/What's There A walk for all seasons. The views are superb so go in clear weather. To the west are the Goyt Valley hills, Greater Manchester, Lantern Pike and Cown Edge. There's a tantalising glimpse of Kinder Reservoir and The Downfall from the north, whilst the Kinder plateau, South Head and Mount Famine dominate the eastern views. Have a good look around the canal basin: Eleven information panels describe the complex and chequered history of this most important inland port of two centuries ago. Limestone from the Dove Holes quarries was lowered on wagons via gravity on the Peak Forest Tramway to be converted into lime at the basin or transported elsewhere on the canal network. Horses pulled the wagons back to the quarries. Gritstone from Chinley Churn quarries was also transported through the basin. Wildlife include raven, buzzard, dipper, partridge, brown hare and stoat and, yes, there is a black swan at a lake near the end!

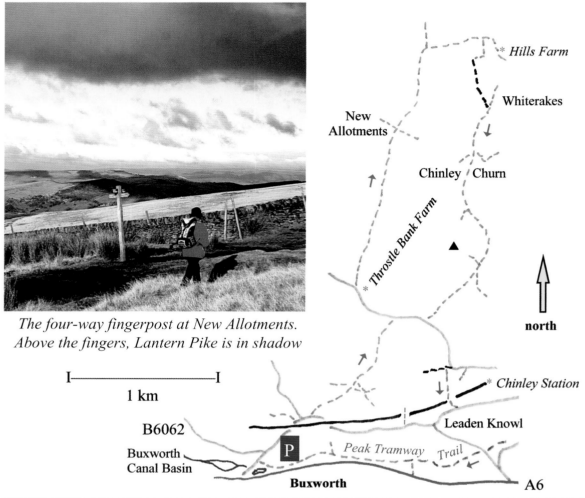

The four-way fingerpost at New Allotments. Above the fingers, Lantern Pike is in shadow

I———————————I

1 km

The path beneath the old quarries along Chinley Churn. Walker's shadow, too! (Nov 7)

Route After having a look around the **Buxworth Canal Basin**, walk east past the *Navigation Inn* entrance to a four-way signpost. Turn sharp left (signed *Buxworth Village*). Cross *Black Brook* to road. Turn right to the B6062. Turn right (signed *Chinley* etc); join pavement on right then cross to pavement on left. Go under railway bridge; pass minor road on left then turn left up path after *Splash Lane End Cottage*. After a few metres, bear right (towards houses) and right again to gate/stile. Follow the walled path. When the way ahead opens out, bear left (over marshy area) up to waymark post. Go ahead, crossing a grassy path up to wall step-stile, right of building. Cross drive; go over stile then, after 20 m, turn left up steps to gate on concession path. Go up to another gate. Continue up path, right of walls to gate and lane. Turn left. Just past **Throstle Bank Farm** turn right up a bridleway to a gate and on to gate/stile. Through, keep ahead as track swings right into field. Ahead is another gate and more access land to **New Allotments**! Soon X-paths are met (fingerposts) but keep ahead. At the top of the hill the path swings right to a junction. Here, go through gate ahead and follow the well-cycled path to a gate. Immediately through, turn right over stile. Follow concession path to gate. Through, bear right uphill then go left to walk above old quarries. As they end, angle left down field to stile/gate. Now follow this grassy path, always ahead to and over another stile and ahead past main quarried section (seat, paths up). Path later falls and narrows to forks. Keep ahead on most worn path down to stile in fence. Keep ahead down through gorse to stile at wall and on down to lane. Turn left. After 400m, turn sharp right after *Stubbins* onto metalled track. After 30m, go through wall-stile on left (picnic tables) and down through park to wall opening; steps and railway footbridge to road. Turn right on pavement then carefully cross road at **Leaden Knowl** and turn left down minor road (signed *Stephanie Works*). Pass works on right; go over bridge (weir) then turn right onto the **Peak Tramway Trail** and follow it back to the canal basin.

South Head from the railway footbridge at Chinley (Nov 7)

Passing a wet spot on the walled rustic path up the west flank of Chinley Churn (Dec 12)

A narrowboat enters Buxworth Canal Basin (Sept 20)

Lyme Hall with The Cage folly above, as seen from Knightslow Wood (Oct 8)

This fine day out starts by crossing the Macclesfield Canal and rises into Lyme Park for a look at the hall. The way then rises up the park to the ancient Bow Stones and expansive views. A scenic descent, passing a café, leads to a level stroll back on the canal towpath.

Length 13 kms / 8.13 miles **Map** O/S Explorer OL1, *Dark Peak Area*, West Sheet
Start/Finish The canal-side car park at Nelson Pit Visitor Centre, 1 km south of Middlewood at SJ 944 833. Buses from Stockport stop at *The Boar's Head*, Shrigley Rd North, Lyme Rd, opposite the Visitor Centre (Cheshire Traveline 0871 200 2233). You could also park in Lyme Park itself (fee) and pick up the walk there at SJ 963 823.
Terrain Tracks and paths with gentle rises. A farmland path is indistinct; may be muddy.
Refreshments The *Coffee Tavern* and the *Boar's Head* pub opposite the Visitor Centre; the *Trading Post* on the towpath and a café just after Birchencliff, about ¾ way round.
When To Go/What's There Go between April and end of October when all the paths are open in Lyme Park (to view hall and fallow deer park). There are about 400 red deer in the park, best seen October/early November when the stags cut their harems from the hind herd. Look either side of the track up to the *Bow Stones*, which are two shafts of Saxon crosses - the crossheads of which are possibly in the courtyard of the Italianate hall, formerly a Tudor house. The hall was *Pemberley* in BBC's adaptation of *Pride and Prejudice*. Daffodils and tulips girdle the hall in spring. Look out for the small herd of Lincoln Red cows on the red deer moor; they have survived as thoroughbred since the 6th century. Other cattle are being introduced to the moor to stem the spread of purple moorgrass, which is dominating the plantlife and impoverishing wildlife, including red deer. A cull of red deer takes place between dusk and 8 am summer months so be out of the park then! The *Coffee Tavern* was built in 1876 by the Poynton Pit owner to keep the miners out of the adjacent *Boar's Head*! Kingfishers and goosanders are often seen at the canal.

I————————I
1 km

P

*Narrowboat livery
shed at the canal*

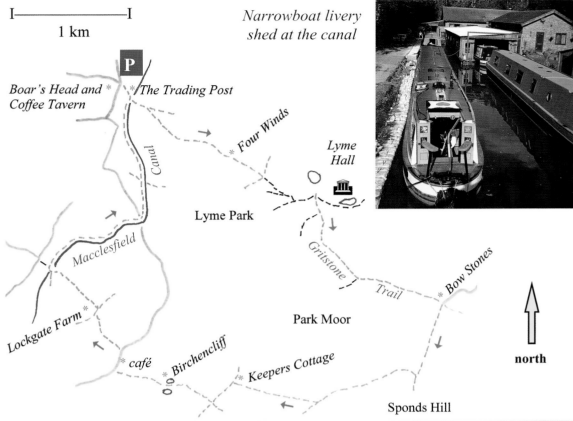

Boar's Head and *
Coffee Tavern

* The Trading Post

Canal

* Four Winds

*Lyme
Hall*

🏛

Lyme Park

Macclesfield

Gritstone

Trail

* Bow Stones

Lockgate Farm *

Park Moor

north

* café * Birchencliff

* Keepers Cottage

Sponds Hill

At The Bow Stones (May 2)

Route Go to the canal and turn right; pass *The Trading Post*; go over cobbled bridge then soon turn right to cross Bridge No 15 over the ***Macclesfield Canal***. Go up the lane, keep ahead at junction and, about 1 km later, at **Four Winds**, enter **Lyme Park** (NT sign). Walk on to join park track and keep ahead to T-junction. Turn left down to another T-junction. Turn right. The route now goes uphill on the ***Gritstone Trail*** but, to have a closer look at Lyme Hall, turn left and go through the gate to the "Fallow Deer Park". Return, and head uphill, right of pines to enter wood via gate. Now, keep ahead on main path to exit wood via gate. Again, keep ahead on main path up to ladder stile after 1 km. Go over to stile. The ***Bow Stones*** are in an enclosure left, but the route turns right; through gate/stile and to another such system after ¾ km. Through, turn right, signed to *Pott Shrigley* (not marked on O/S map). Follow path left of wall. After about 1 km, main path bears left to stile/wooden gate-posts. Go through and immediately head right, up to stile, well left of wall. Follow path down, left of wall; through gate near bottom of field and on through opening to track at ***Keepers Cottage***. Turn left. After about 300m turn right through gate and follow bridleway down to between the lakes of ***Birchencliff***; its cottages on the right and down to a minor road. Turn right. Pass café on right and, 250 m later, turn left across road at right bend on path signed *Poynton*. Go through two gates then, half-way across the long field, leave the hedge on the left and bear right to buildings. Ignore stile left, but go over twin stile right of house. After 20m turn left and go over two stiles to meet farm track of ***Lockgate Farm***. Follow track ahead. It crosses the Macclesfield Canal via bridge (No 18). After a few metres turn right on to towpath. Turn left; 3 kms later walk under bridge No 15 to car.

Having a peep at Italianate Lyme Hall from the path to the fallow deer park (April 12)

Red deer in Lyme Park; seen from the path up to the Bow Stones (Oct 8)

The Trading Post also offers day boat hire on the canal (www.canaltradingpost.com)

Walks On Dark Peak Map ———————— East Sheet

(Explorer Outdoor Leisure Series No 01)

At the top of Ditch Clough (Walk 19, Oct 10)

15 Harden Reservoir, Lower Snailsden Moss and Winscar Reservoir

Winscar Reservoir from the shoulder of Dearden Spring (March 21)

On the O/S map, this walk around Harden and Winscar Reservoirs looks as though it would be just an easy stroll beside the water. The east leg of the route is; but the south and west legs, where few tread, is over rough moor and access land - but it's well worth the extra effort to enjoy some fine scenery and solitude away from the car park visitors.

Length 9 kms / 5.63 miles **Map** O/S Explorer OL1, *Dark Peak Area*, East Sheet
Start/Finish Dunford Bridge car park on the Trans Pennine Trail at SE 158 024. Here, there is also a bus stop where buses from the Holmfirth, Barnsley, Sheffield and Penistone areas stop (routes 20 and 57: Travelines 01709 515151: 0871 2002233). Those with cars could start at Broad Hill car park and avoid the 1 km round trip of up and down the headwall of Winscar Reservoir (see sketch and O/S map).
Terrain Easy tracks and a little roadwork followed by a lot of undulating moor on access land where, as the route is not often undertaken, the paths are very narrow and indistinct in places. The route involves easily avoiding a property and fields not on access land.
Refreshments *The Stanhope* bar and restaurant at Dunford Bridge may be open.
When To Go/What's There A walk for all seasons but at its best after a few dry days and when the heather is in bloom. On summer weekends the Pennine Sailing Club add a splash of colour to Winscar Reservoir. As you pass through Broad Hill car park you will be greeted by dozens of mallards, Canada geese and a host of hybrid waterfowl scrounging for food. Many limp after too eager a rush towards an incoming car! Other birds include kestrel, buzzard, curlew, snipe, lapwing, skylark, cormorant, grey wagtail and oystercatcher. There are mountain hares, stoats, lizards and common hawker dragonflies. Tormentil, foxglove, marsh pennywort, bilberry, crowberry, eyebright, cross-leaved heath and cotton-grasses flower. Butterflies include small white, green hairstreak, small heath, green-veined white and peacock. The headwall of Winscar is heather-clad.

Fording the River Don (Aug 24) **Inset.** *Oystercatchers on headwall of Harden Reservoir*

An alternative track crosses Swiner Clough (above) and also leads to the ford across the River Don (see "Route"). Here, beside the ancient Scots Pines, is a fine place for lunch.

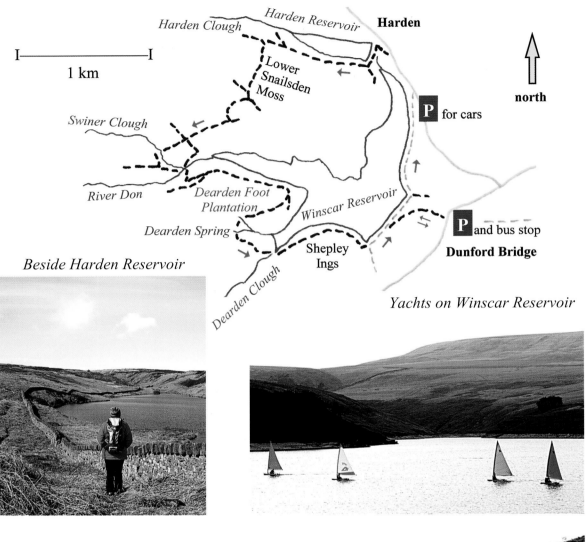

Beside Harden Reservoir

Yachts on Winscar Reservoir

Approaching Dearden Foot Plantation (Aug 24)

Route Walk out of the car park, cross the road and go up *Don View*. Go through metal gate on right and, after barrier, bear left up the headwall of ***Winscar Reservoir*** to the top. Turn right. Bear left at end of headwall; pass through a car park and go up to road. Bear left. After 400m, and before houses at **Harden**, turn left down track; go through gate and cross headwall of ***Harden Reservoir***. Turn right. Follow 4x4 track up beside the reservoir. Ignore fork down right. About 100m before a ruin ahead, another track is met. Here, turn 90° left. Keep ahead as track joins on right. Track rises over **Lower Snailsden Moss** then, as it starts to descend and before a left bend, bear right a little on faint track and pass through old gateposts. Follow track down to wall and entrance. Don't go through but follow just right of the wall as it soon curves down to a track. Turn right. After about 400m the track forks and you have two options: either take the left track and follow it down to ford the ***River Don*** or (more adventurous), take the middle track through the gateposts and down through a pine wood to cross the stream in ***Swiner Clough***. The track doglegs left then right. Here, leave track and bear left down the shoulder of the clough to stream. Turn left and cross stream. Now follow left bank of River Don downstream for 50m to ford. Routes are now joined. After fording follow track up. It turns sharp left then, as it turns sharp right, walk ahead on a narrower track. This track undulates and passes grouse butts on the right then, at fork, go left down towards the reservoir and the pines of **Dearden Foot Plantation**. After start of trees path forks. Bear right, away from pines, and path rises and later bears right to cross two issues of ***Dearden Spring***. Immediately after the marshy second, turn left down the shoulder and head down to the inlet of the south-west arm of the reservoir. Cross the stream at a suitable point and turn left, following the path nearest the water. Later it becomes more distinct. Just before sailing club boats, it is wise to leave path up right to cross eroded gully at the top. Over, return to path. At end of fence path turns 90° left down to gate. Cross to headwall. After 100m, bear right to **Dunford Bridge**.

Watching the sailing from the SW inlet to Winscar Reservoir from Dearden Clough

16 Langsett Reservoir, Mickleden Edge and Pike Lowe

Approaching the summit cairn on Pike Lowe (Aug 19). It used to be higher.

Now on access land, Pike Lowe is open for visitors! Our fairly tough outing starts beside Langsett Reservoir; rises to Mickleden Edge and crosses Reddle Pits Ridge to the peak.

Length 13 kms / 8.13 miles **Map** O/S Explorer OL1, *Dark Peak Area*, East Sheet
Start/Finish Car park at Langsett Reservoir Ranger Centre and picnic site off the A616 at SE 210 004. There is a limited bus service to the centre. Ask for Manchester Road / Midhope Cliff Lane. Traveline 01709 51 51 51. Web site : travelsouthyorkshire.com
Terrain From the reservoir to Mickleden Edge the walk is on easy to follow paths. The trek across the moor to Pike Lowe is mainly on a shooters' path. The descent from Pike Lowe to the reservoir is over rough moorland. You may encounter the odd grough and do avoid the green *Sphagna* bogs. There is a short but quite steep path near the end of the walk. Be skilled in map and compass and accustomed to walking over rough terrain.
Refreshments None en route. *Bank Top Café* and *Wagon & Horses Inn* near to car park
When To Go/What's There Go after a dry period; in good visibility and, for the most picturesque views, when the heather is in flower. So that should narrow it down a bit! The Ranger Centre is not always open, even in summer, but the local weather forecast is usually displayed. The walk crosses access land which is closed when grouse shooting takes place. Phone the Open Access Contact Centre on 0845 100 3298 to see when. The heather is burnt in patches on a 15-year or so cycle to generate new growth for grouse. We have seen buzzard, kestrel, merlin, short-eared owl and peregrine falcon. On hot summer days lizards bask on the paths. Mountain hares are most often seen in winter. As well as red grouse; golden plover, curlew and meadow pipit also frequent the moors. The lower bogs support creeping spearwort and marsh pennywort. There are small stands of bell heather, cross-leaved heath, crowberry and gorse as well as tasty bilberries to pick.

Through the pines beside Langsett Reservoir at the start of the walk (Sept 30)

Crossing a grough on the way to Reddle Pits Ridge and Pike Lowe (Aug 19)

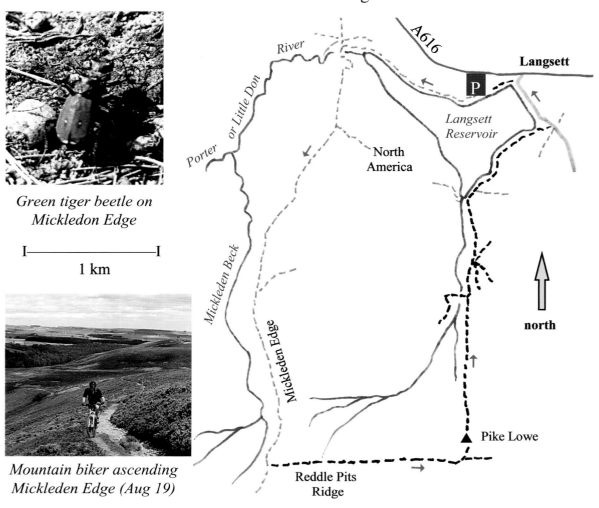

Green tiger beetle on Mickledon Edge

I————————I
1 km

Mountain biker ascending Mickleden Edge (Aug 19)

Starting the waterside path near the end of the walk (Aug 19)

Route From the car park, walk down to the reservoir and turn right. Stay on the waterside path for about 1½ kms to the end of the reservoir. Path rises to junction. Bear left and left again at another junction. Cross the bridge over **Little Don River**; bear left; go through gate and follow path which snakes uphill then straightens to meet path on left (to **North America**!). Keep ahead on path which undulates through the heather and bilberry moor to reach another path on the left after about 1¾ kms. Again, keep ahead as path rises over **Mickleden Edge**. Path widens near head of clough and passes cairn. After paved sections, path joins a watercourse and generally keeps left of it to meet another cairn. From this second cairn, look left (90° due east) and you will see the mound of **Pike Lowe**, about 1½ kms away. However, continue up path for another 100m or so, then go left onto the moor. Find the crest of the moor which is **Reddle Pits Ridge**. Here is a shooters' path which runs 120° beside occasional wooden posts and leads to the right flank of Pike Lowe. On the way a stone post is passed with *RRW* on its face; *B* on the reverse and a cross on the top. After the stone, path forks but keep ahead for about another 200m then leave the path and walk left up to the summit cairn. From the summit, head down north, heading towards a distinctive path you can see leading to **Langsett Reservoir**. Keep right of a watercourse. As you get lower, keep right to avoid much of the bracken and soft rush and head down soggy ground to meet the track (photo below). Bear right and, where two other tracks join from the right, keep ahead (left) for about another 40m then leave the track on the left on a narrow concession path which heads towards a pine wood. From here, follow path ahead, left of fence to wooden "stile" on right. Don't go over, but go ahead on path between wall and fence down to a gate and a wide track. Cross track and go right on the narrow waterside path. Path enters wood and reaches waymark post. Here, go left on narrow waterside path to fence. Bear right, steeply uphill, then left, following fence. Here are the fine aerial views of Langsett Reservoir. The path finally falls and, as it bears left about 100m from the headwall road, the path forks. Bear right to opening between wall and fence. Turn left, walk on right side of road then cross headwall on pavement on left. Immediately after, turn left through gate beside overflow steps. After about 150m, turn sharp right at a junction up to the car park.

The welcome sight of the track after the arduous, off-path descent of Pike Lowe (Aug 19)

17 Wortley Top Forge, Thurgoland Tunnel and Tin Mill Rocher

One of the two optional sets of stepping stones across the River Don (Sept 2)

This hidden gem just to the north of Stocksbridge has many variants. To get the best out of the walk: Visit the old forge; go through the tunnel (with company); ply the paths over Green Moor and return via Tin Mill Rocher and stepping stones across the R. Don.

Length 8 kms / 5 miles **Map** O/S Explorer OL1, *Dark Peak Area*, East Sheet
Start/Finish Car Park on the Upper Don Trail, 1 km west of Wortley at SK 299 993.
Buses run from Barnsley and Penistone to the forge (Travel S Yorks 01709 515151)
Terrain A mix of tracks, paths and a little roadwork. Some uphill but not too strenuous.
Refreshments *The Bridge Inn* appears just after Wortley Top Forge.
When To Go/What's There Go on a Sunday in early May when the bluebells in Tin Mill Woods are in bloom and when Wortley Top Forge is open. There is an entrance fee, but if you have kids the admission fee includes a trip on a miniature railway. It leaves about 2 pm. As this is a fairly short walk, you could start around lunchtime; visit the forge; go on the train; lunch at the *Bridge Inn* and then walk it off during the 4 miles that follow! The 17th century forge is the oldest surviving water-powered heavy iron forge to retain its original waterwheels, hammers and cranes (info 0114 288 7576; www.topforge.co.uk). Also for us kids (at heart) is the Thurgoland Tunnel on the Trans Pennine Trail. Go with company and take a torch in case of power failure. In the tunnel let rip with some shrieks and listen to the amazing echoes reverberating upwards of ten seconds. There is graffiti here and the whole experience can be quite spooky! The walk proper starts after the tunnel and leads under a viaduct with the delightful name of Rumtickle Viaduct. Optional stepping stones and a set of stocks with a fine viewpoint provide more interest. Dipper and grey wagtail are on the river, buzzard in the sky and warblers sing in spring. In summer the diverse wayside flowers attract at least ten species of butterfly.

Top. *Ready for the Thurgoland Tunnel experience? At the entrance of the tunnel. Remember, don't go alone and take a torch in case of power failure and to be seen by horse riders and cyclists. But don't forget to let rip and enjoy the echoes!*

Left. *On the path over Green Moor Delf (Sept 26)*

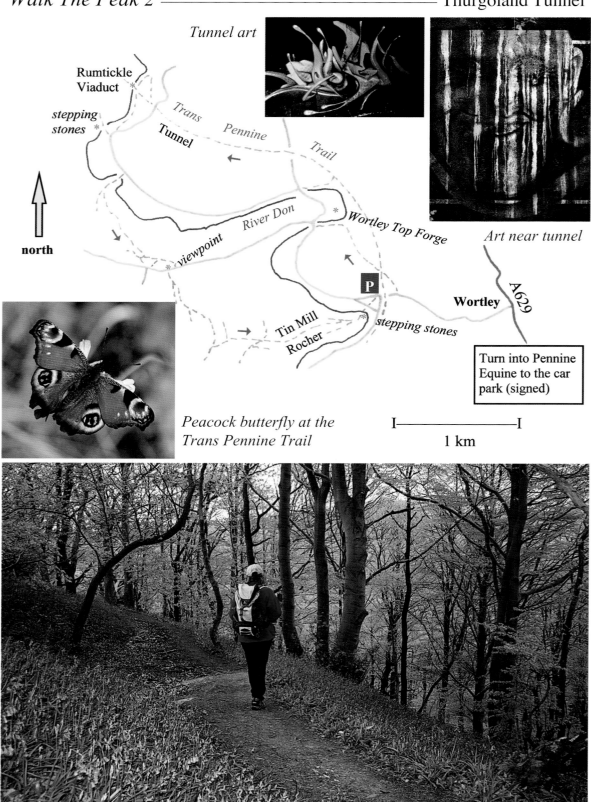

Tunnel art

Rumtickle
Viaduct

stepping
stones

Trans Pennine Trail

Tunnel

north

River Don

viewpoint

Wortley Top Forge

Art near tunnel

P

Wortley

A629

Tin Mill
Rocher

stepping stones

Turn into Pennine
Equine to the car
park (signed)

*Peacock butterfly at the
Trans Pennine Trail*

I————————I
1 km

On the path through the top of Tin Mill Rocher Woods (May 9)

Route Turn left out of the car park then bear left down to *Upper Don Trail*. Cross and go up path slanting right to bridge. Turn left on path running right of wall and follow it down to bottom of long field. Here, bear left and go between buildings then turn left on track to road. Turn right and go over bridge across the ***River Don***. Keep right at junction (signed *Thurgoland*). Soon ***Wortley Top Forge*** is on the right. On, follow pavement, cross river again then immediately turn right down steps. (The *Bridge Inn* is a little up the road from here). Go ahead on riverside path, through kissing gate then turn left at fork away from river. Go left at another fork. At T-junction turn left uphill. Keep left of tunnel on right and go up steps to the ***Trans Pennine Trail***. Turn left. After a km go through ***Thurgoland Tunnel***. After exiting, go under bridge and, after 40m, turn right and go over stile ahead and follow path down to river. Turn left over stile and follow path under Rumtickle Viaduct. Go over stile and ahead on riverside path and up to wall stile left of gate. Immediately turn right over stile and go ahead to stile and a lane. Turn right. (If you want more stepping stones, turn right after 80m and follow path to river then return). 300m up the lane, turn right over wall at first footpath sign and go over footbridge ahead. Follow path ahead through copse to field. Here, keep left (not up to gate on right) and on to stile complex left of gate. Over, follow track ahead and up until it hairpins right. Here, leave track and walk ahead. Keep ahead at second waymark post and walk on up to gate and stile. Over, follow path by house to road. Turn right. After 80m, there are stocks on the right and a green with seats and ***viewpoint***. Opposite the green, go up metalled track. Turn left at info board. After 100m turn left on another path. At fork ahead keep left on main path. At another fork, go left then, after seat on right and, as path bends right, turn left on narrower path up steps to stile. Over, walk ahead over field to stile left of gate. Keep ahead, go beneath power lines, cross track and go over stile ahead. Follow path along hillside. When it joins another path bear left then go through gate entrance on right. Walk down wooden steps into woods of **Tin Mill Rocher**. Go ahead and later, at wall corner on left, also keep ahead then down to T-junction. Turn left down to footbridge (or stepping stones) across river and on up to lane. Cross. Go over stile and on to another then up steps to road. Turn left to T-junction. Cross road, go up track then soon turn right up to the *Trans Pennine Trail*. Turn left. After 100m turn right to the car park.

Balancing-act on Tin Mill Stepping Stones (Sept 26)

Broomhead Moor, Hurkling Edge and Canyards Hills SSSI

Resting at the Hurkling Stones **Inset.** *Larva of oak eggar moth seen here (both Aug 2).*

This walk full of interest starts with a stroll to Ewden Beck stone circle then encircles Broomhead Moor to Hurkling Edge and an aircraft wreck. The Hurkling Stones are passed followed by a most unusual roadside milestone on the way to the geologically unique and ecologically fragile Site of Special Scientific Interest at Canyards Hills.

Length 11 kms / 6.88 miles **Map** O/S Explorer OL1, *Dark Peak Area*, East Sheet
Start/Finish Off-road parking area for about half a dozen cars opposite Broomhead Hall and where the public footpath to Ewden Beck starts at SK 241 962.
Terrain Apart from the short section of uphill track to the shooting cabin on Broomhead Moor, this is a mostly level walk on tracks and paths. There is a short off-path half km to the path along Hurkling Edge and a full km round trip off-path to the Wellington wreck.
Refreshments None on route.
When To Go/What's There The few hectares of Canyards Hills SSSI pack in a wealth of wildlife at the hummocks and pools. One pool supports rafts of *Sphagnum* moss, abundant bogbean (scarce in The Peak), marsh pennywort, black darter and four-spot chaser dragonflies; others have whirlygig beetles, pond skaters, water boatmen, branched bur-reed, spike-rush, pondweed, emerald damselflies and common darters. Herons hunt for frogs and newts. Wreckage of the Wellington bomber that came down on Broomhead Moor on 9 December 1942 lies at SK 23476 95416 (GPS ref. acc. 4m). The crew survived. Ewden Beck "stone circle" lies at SK 23820 96651, but it needs a leap of faith to visualize the circle - perhaps for enthusiasts only. The moors have bilberry, cowberry and cross-leaved heath as well as ling heather and associated red grouse. Buzzards soar overhead. This area has a few unique milestones (see p.92 with more on p.235). Curlew and lapwing call in spring and waders may be spotted in autumn, reservoir-bound. Ancient tree root systems and moor club fungi are in the peat after the shooting lodge.

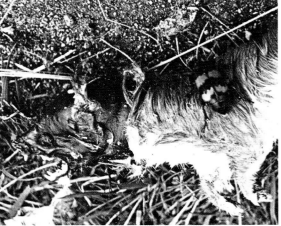

Left. *Wildlife pool at Canyards Hills in the autumn (Oct 24).*

Above. *Burying beetle getting to work on a weasel corpse on Hurkling Edge. After burying the carcase the female lays her eggs so that the hatched larvae ...(yuk)*

Below. *In Canyards Hills SSSI where,* **Left Inset***, cow-wheat and,* **Right Inset***, bell heather, are abundant (all Aug 2).*

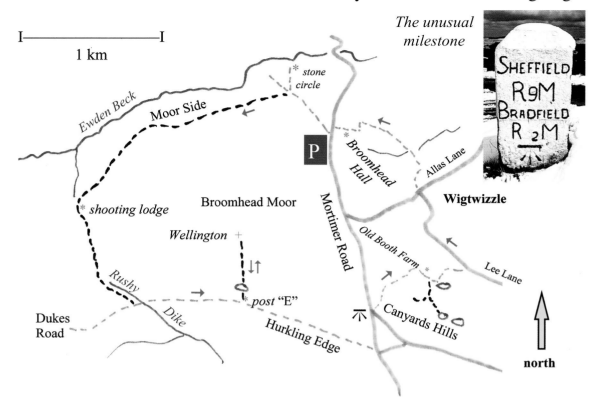

The unusual milestone

SHEFFIELD R 9M BRADFIELD R 2M

1 km

Ewden Beck

Moor Side

* stone circle

* Broomhead Hall

Allas Lane

Wigtwizzle

P

Broomhead Moor

* shooting lodge

Wellington +

Mortimer Road

Old Booth Farm *

Lee Lane

* post "E"

Rushy Dike

Dukes Road

Hurkling Edge

Canyards Hills

north

At the Wellington crash site on Broomhead Moor. **Inset.** *The salubrious shooting lodge.*

Route Go through the gate and follow the track. After about 250 m, at bends, a footpath sign is reached on the right. To see the ***stone circle*** – don't take the distinct path immediately left of the post but take the path immediately right of the post. The start may be obscured by bracken. Follow path for about 150m. The circle lies about 15m beyond a conspicuous marker post. Return to track and follow this most pleasant of paths over **Moor Side**. Further on it weaves up to the ***shooting lodge***.

Continue on path beyond the lodge until it fizzles out then angle half left to a watercourse (***Rushy Dike***) and follow it (bearing 120° SE) for about 300m or so to meet a path. Turn left. Soon a wall on the right begins. After about 250m there is a small stone post on the left. The south face is inscribed *RHRW*; the north ***E*** (important as other posts lettered differently on north face). Here, if you want to visit the ***Wellington*** site turn left at the post (small pool beyond) and walk north for about 400m then use GPS. If you haven't one, you may spot what appears to be a slanting grave stone, inscribed *Deakins Moorhall*. The wreckage lies 96° E and 50m away. Return, continue along **Hurkling Edge**, passing the Hurkling Stones to reach a road. Turn left. Pass fenced O/S datum point on left to milepost on right at junction. Go through gate ahead and down track. Opposite ***Old Booth Farm*** is the access gate to **Canyards Hills** if you wish to visit. Return and continue on track which doglegs to meet a road (**Lee Lane**). Turn left to meet T-junction. Turn right then immediately go over wall step-stile on left. Ahead, cross two streams and, at waymark post, bear right as directed to stile/gate at wall. Keep ahead to gate and cross stream to gate/stile. Head up field right of fence to wall step-stile right of dwelling. Over, turn left to another wall step-stile then turn right to road and parking area.

An unusual ice-particle bow from the path beside Broomhead Hall (Jan 18)

19 West End to Alport Castles, Ravens Clough and Westend Clough

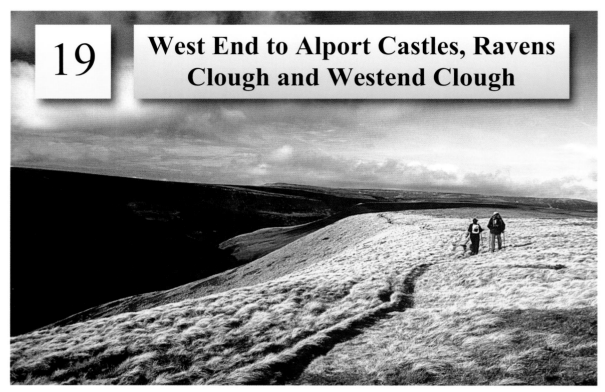

On the path high above Alport Dale to the trig pillar (Feb 7)

Although Walk The Peak also visited Alport Castles, this shorter approach leads to an (optional) exhilarating trek to the wild, scenic delights of Ravens Clough and the River Westend tumbling down from the Bleaklow plateau. A hidden gem of the Upper Derwent.

Length 10 kms / 6.25 miles **Map** O/S Explorer OL1, *Dark Peak Area*, East Sheet
Start/Finish Parking for about a dozen cars around West End bus stop at SK 154 927.
If full, you could park at Fairholmes and take the bus. Bus times (Route 222) fluctuate
so ring the visitor centre beforehand (01433 650953). The road to West End bus stop is
closed to cars on Sundays and Bank Holiday Mondays, from Fairholmes northwards.
Terrain It's hard going from the trig pillar off-path to Ravens Clough. Birchin Hat to the
trig pillar can be boggy after rain. There are several steep descents and care has to be
taken crossing the streams and River Westend. You must be skilled in map and compass.
Refreshments None on route. Fairholmes visitor centre has hot/cold snacks when open.
When To Go/What's There Go after a period of dry weather as the crux of the walk is
the crossing of the River Westend - tricky even then! Views up to the Castles include the
Grinah Stones, Barrow Stones, Crow Stones, Bull Stones and Dovestone Tor; plus the
trig pillars on Margery Hill and Back Tor. The view into Alport Dale is awesome and the
entire Kinder Scout plateau is revealed. Birds include goshawk, kestrel, peregrine falcon,
wheatear, red grouse and meadow pipits on the moor and, in the woods, goldcrest and the
occasional crossbill. The flora is mainly heather, moor grasses and bilberry with a little
cross-leaved heath and tormentil. Bracken continues to invade. Marshy areas have water
forget-me-not, marsh willow-herb and marsh ragwort. There are red lichens on Birchin
Hat. The real floral interest is near the end of the walk where a conservation area supports
bog asphodel, marsh pennywort, sneezewort, greater bird's-foot trefoil, marsh thistle and
marsh-orchids. Pools support pond skaters, water-crowfoot and water crickets.

Top Left. *The path up Ditch Clough Plantation (Nov 14).*

Top Right. *Red admiral butterfly on heather at the landslip knoll (Aug 2).*

Above. *The landmark sheepfold beside the River Westend.*

Right. *Looking up the River Westend from the landslip knoll after crossing the river (Aug 2).*

Below. *On the diminutive path above Ravens Clough (Aug 2).*

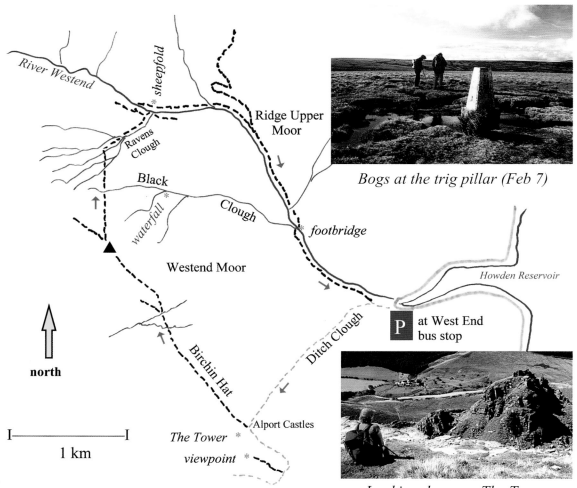

Bogs at the trig pillar (Feb 7)

River Westend

*sheepfold

Ridge Upper Moor

Ravens Clough

Black

Clough

waterfall

*footbridge

Howden Reservoir

▲

Westend Moor

Ditch Clough

P at West End bus stop

north

Birchin Hat

I———————I

1 km

Alport Castles

The Tower *

viewpoint *

Looking down on The Tower

The Tower at Alport Castles from the viewpoint (Aug 7)

Route Go through the gate next to the bus stop. After a short distance leave the main track and turn left up a path (signpost) which steadily rises through Ditch Clough Plantation. It continues to rise after the woods but levels out at the head of **Ditch Clough** and soon leads to the view above **Alport Castles**. If you wish to go to the viewpoint, turn left and a path leads downhill to a break in a wall which gives access to the **viewpoint**. You will then have to walk back up! From the top a path runs right of a wall along **Birchin Hat** and above Alport Dale. After a second watercourse, the path forks. Go right and another km or so leads to the trig pillar on **Westend Moor**. Now walk north, off-path, for about a km - don't be tempted to turn right down **Black Clough** but battle on until you have negotiated about 4 groughs in quick succession. If you have GPS, you want to be at about SK 128 941. Now set your compass to 40° and angle down right until you are above the deep cleft of **Ravens Clough**. Turn left and cross the stream higher up the clough. Rise a little and a faint path is met which runs NE. Follow this until you are high above the **River Westend** and can see the **sheepfold** (photo) far below. Don't be seduced by the path which runs right, down to the confluence of the Westend and Ravens Brook and above the right bank of the Westend, but turn left and follow the path as it loses height until a swathe of marsh is seen running down to the river. Descend to the river, keeping just right of the marsh. Turn left, upstream, where it is possible to cross the river in a few places before the first tree. Climb up from the river to the top of a landslip knoll, where there is a path along the crest and a fine view of the river tumbling down from Bleaklow (photo). From here, a faint path leads to a more distinct path higher up the hillside. Follow this downstream. There is one more narrow stream to cross. Where paths divide, keep on the one closest the river. Two stiles give access and exit to a fenced conservation area and the path now leads up to the track coming down from **Ridge Upper Moor**. Turn right and follow the track which forks after about a km. Go left, cross the **footbridge** and walk back to the start.

Contemplating crossing the River Westend. **Inset.** *Bog asphodel growing downstream.*

20 | Ughill Moors, Lodge Moor, Boot's Folly and Strines Reservoirs

Looking to Derwent Edge from the start of Ughill Moors (Aug 27)

The striking and prominent landmark of Boot's Folly can be seen from many vistas in the Strines area as it sits loftily above Strines Reservoir. We visit the tower after a trip over Ughill Moors with their expansive views. A full circuit of Dale Dike Reservoir follows.

Length 12 kms / 7.5 miles **Map** O/S Explorer OL1, *Dark Peak Area*, East Sheet
Start/Finish Off-road parking on Wet Shaw Lane where the track of Stake Hill Road starts at SK 245 904. Only feasible public transport is bus 273 from Sheffield to Moscar Top (SK 231 879) and walk in via Moscar Lodge and pick up walk from Lodge Moor. This will add about 2kms to the walk. South Yorkshire buses/trains 01709 515 151.
Terrain An easy route to follow but some sections, particularly from the tower down to Dale Dike Reservoir can be very boggy after rain - as can the waterside paths.
Refreshments None on route.
When To Go/What's There A few mountain hares have expanded their range to Lodge Moor and Ughill Moors and, as brown hares also roam the pastures, this is one of only a few walks where both species may be seen. Lapwing, curlew and skylark perform above. Woodland supports green and great spotted woodpecker, nuthatch, long-tailed tit and squirrel. Most populous water birds are mallard and Canada geese with a few resident greylag geese. Moorhen, coot and a few tufted duck add a little variety. Game birds include red grouse, pheasant, snipe, and we once saw a woodcock. Foxgloves are abundant as is tormentil. The metal window frames have fallen from the tower as have a few crown blocks, so don't venture too close! The tower was constructed to keep local men in work during a depression, which was a fine gesture by the landowner in austere times. There is a short guide stoop at the start of the walk with hard to read script and another after Moscar Lodge, which you will meet if you opt for the bus. It has a benchmark and Hope, Sheffield, Bradfield and Hathersage inscribed on its four aspects.

98

Top. *At a low Dale Dike Reservoir*

Above. *On the descent from Lodge Moor to Sugworth Road, with Boot's Folly ahead (both Oct 18)*

Left. *Bents House from Sugworth Road, with Back Tor on Derwent Edge above (Aug 27)*

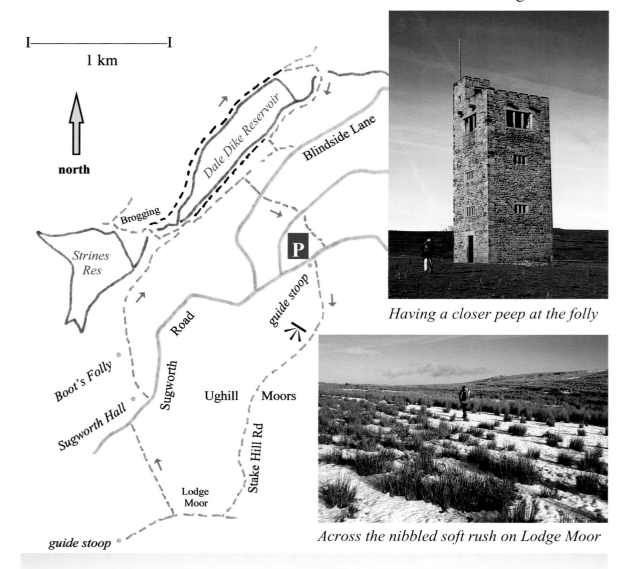

I———————I
1 km

north

Dale Dike Reservoir

Blindside Lane

Brogging

Strines
Res

P

guide stoop *

Road

Boot's Folly *

Sugworth

Sugworth Hall *

Ughill : Moors

Stake Hill Rd

Lodge
Moor

guide stoop *

Having a closer peep at the folly

Across the nibbled soft rush on Lodge Moor

Strines Reservoir from near to Boot's Folly (Oct 18)

Route Try and decipher the script on the **guide stoop** then go through the gate. Walk up the track (**Stake Hill Road**). As it bends right, there's a **benchmark** on a walled-in stone gatepost on the right. Through a gate and the heather on **Ughill Moor** appears. At the highest point of the track, The Great Ridge, Winhill Pike, Stanage End and Derwent Edge are viewed. After a second gate a track joins from the left. About 70m after a third gate turn right over wall stile. Ahead, over and down **Lodge Moor** and a couple of stile/gates leads to a wall stile and **Sugworth Road**. Turn right. Take the steps left of the gates to *Sugworth Hall*; walk down drive until directed right, through a tunnel of rhododendron to emerge on open ground after stile/gate. Path runs right of *Boot's Folly* and down past waymark posts, turns sharp left at fencing and continues down past some wonderful old stone gateposts to the valley bottom, where there is a wall stile after bearing left. Over, go ahead (path right is your return route). As the path forks, go right and over footbridge across outflow from **Strines Reservoir**. Now follow permissive waterside path all the way to gates left of headwall. Walk ahead on track then turn sharp right at a junction. Track runs through woods; over bridge and leads to steps left of outflow pipes of **Dale Dike Reservoir**. More steps lead to the waterside path and a seat. Follow this permissive path to the end of the reservoir and at a waymark post turn sharp left to the wall stile in the valley bottom again. Over, bear left and keep just right of a wall to stile. Over, go down to and cross stream at Holes Wood (conservation area and picnic table). More fields and stiles lead to another picnic table and the conservation area of Andrew Wood (information board). More fields lead to a pine wood. Don't enter, but turn 90° right up a path which is indistinct at first as it rises steeply up rocky terrain. Keep as close to the fence on your left as possible to a ladder stile at a road, **Blindside Lane**. Cross, and walk ahead to another ladder stile and road. Cross, and follow the path ahead to yet another road. Turn right to the start of the walk.

A rainbow over the tower that is Boot's Folly. How an ageing man ran for this shot!

The Seven Stones of Hordron, Lead Hill and Ladybower Woods NR

The path down from Whinstone Lee Tor to Fairholmes (Aug 27)

This half-day walk with only gentle uphill sections first circuits Hordron Edge to visit the enigmatic Seven Stones of Hordron stone circle. From Cutthroat Bridge the way leads across moors to Whinstone Lee Tor and magnificent views. A traverse of Lead Hill brings more aerial views of Ladybower Reservoir before we descend to the nature reserve in Ladybower Woods. This is an on-route optional detour accounted for in the route length.

Length 10 kms / 6.25 miles **Map** O/S Explorer OL1, *Dark Peak Area*, East Sheet
Start/Finish A substantial lay-by on the A57 north of Bamford at SK 216 874. There is also room for about 5 cars at Cutthroat Bridge, the start of the walk proper, should you be an early riser. Buses stop both at the lay-by and the *Ladybower Inn*, also on route.
Terrain Largely moorland paths and tracks. Some will be muddy after rain (see p.14).
Refreshments The *Ladybower Inn*, just a few metres detour, is usually open all day.
When To Go/What's There A walk for all seasons. But it is the panoramic views from Whinstone Lee Tor and Lead Hill which most impress the walker: Bamford Edge, Win Hill, The Great Ridge, Crook Hill, Kinder Scout and the Upper Derwent appear from left to right, so go on a clear day. The heather in flower colours the scenery but the autumn hues are just as picturesque. There are natural basins atop the *Hurkling Stones* where Ladybower Tor can just be seen to the south. Here, off-route yet on access land, are two ancient carvings on a slab at SK 2045 8695 (Barnatt & Robinson, 2003). With the *Seven Stones of Hordron* stone circle being just over the valley, there was almost certain to have been an association. Pagan art and other offerings are frequently left at the circle. Most of the wildlife on the walk is to be found in Ladybower Woods, one of a small number of upland sessile oak woods left in The Peak. The reserve is managed by the Derbyshire Wildlife Trust and is a haven for fungi, mosses, lichens, wood ants, birds and butterflies.

After exceptionally late snow at the Seven Stones of Hordron (April 17, 2008) and ...

... after an exceptional autumn storm! (Oct 29) **Top Inset.** *Pagan art left at the site.*

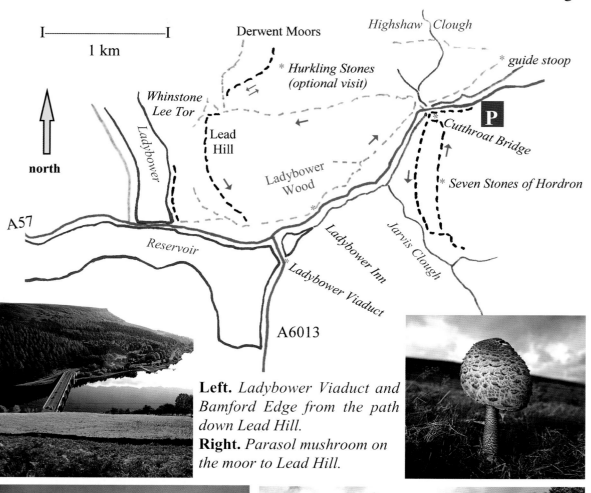

I————————I
1 km

north

Derwent Moors

Highshaw *Clough*

* *Hurkling Stones (optional visit)*

* *guide stoop*

Whinstone Lee Tor

Ladybower

Lead Hill

P

Cutthroat Bridge

Ladybower Wood

* *Seven Stones of Hordron*

A57

Reservoir

Ladybower Inn

Jarvis Clough

* *Ladybower Viaduct*

A6013

Left. *Ladybower Viaduct and Bamford Edge from the path down Lead Hill.*
Right. *Parasol mushroom on the moor to Lead Hill.*

On the path up to Hordron Edge **Left.** *(Jan 19);* **Right.** *(Oct 29)*

Route From the lay-by, walk west downhill for about 250 metres on the narrow path of the left verge of the **A57** to **Cutthroat Bridge**. Turn left over the stile where an access land sign should be also present. The track ahead runs pleasantly up betwixt Scots pine and larch trees and to the left of **Jarvis Clough**. The track then runs more steeply uphill to breach Hordron Edge. Here, a less distinct track/path runs left along the edge so leave the main track and follow this new path for about half a kilometre until the *Seven Stones of Hordron* stone circle comes into view, just to the right of the track. Return to the path and continue along the edge. After the last rocky outcrop it is possible to descend from the edge (no path) and walk down to and through the wood to reach the track and stile again. Carefully cross the A57 (traffic is fast here) and go through the gate. Follow the stony path up and over the moor. For years this was a most pleasant journey but mountain bikers have gradually churned up much of the path (see page 14). After just over a kilometre and at the head of the moor, path junctions are reached, but walk ahead past them to the grassy platform and the fabulous view from **Whinstone Lee Tor**. Now, if you want to top the *Hurkling Stones*, backtrack a few metres and turn uphill where a narrow path leaves the main path to reach them on the right. Return to viewpoint and turn left (south) on a path that runs along the crest of **Lead Hill**, passing more fine viewpoints of **Ladybower Reservoir** and beyond. The path runs steeply down to join another. Keep ahead and soon a signed path leads right to the *Ladybower Inn*, should you wish. Ahead, the path runs below **Ladybower Wood**. After a couple of gates, a path leads left into the reserve (optional) or ahead to Cutthroat Bridge.

Ladybower Reservoir and Derwent Dam east tower from Lead Hill (Nov 16).
Inset. *The boulder is initialled and has these unusual "drill" holes at one end.*

22 Redmires Reservoirs, The Head Stone and Wyming Brook SSSI

On the path beside Upper Redmires Reservoir (July 28)

This short and fairly easy amble first runs beside Redmires Reservoirs, then rises to a viewpoint and heads across moors to the isolated Head Stone. Wyming Brook Drive track then leads to a picturesque ascent of Wyming Brook itself as it winds its way up the dell.

Length 9 kms / 5.63 miles **Map** O/S Explorer OL1, *Dark Peak Area*, East Sheet **Start/Finish** Wyming Brook Nature Reserve car park off Redmires Road at SK 269 858. Number 51 buses from Sheffield terminate at the bottom of Soughley Lane on Redmires Road, which is virtually at the start of the walk (see map). Traveline 01709 51 51 51.
Terrain An easy route to follow on paths and tracks. Care needed up Wyming Brook.
Refreshments None
When To Go/ What's There A walk for all seasons. Although there are three fairly large reservoirs, the aquatic bird life is rather impoverished having only the usual Canada goose colony etc. However, we have seen the odd common sandpiper on the shoreline. The drains beside the reservoirs are more alive, having bog pondweed and water-crowfoot, and support frogs, newts, great diving beetles, large red damselflies and common hawker dragonflies. Lapwings, curlews and skylarks delight us with their calls and antics in spring and summer. And, you will definitely get buzzed by curlews if you ascend the viewpoint at nesting-time! The SSSI woods of Wyming Brook support tree pipits, goldcrest, crossbill, blackcap, woodcock and woodpeckers and dozens of fungi in autumn. Look out for weasels around the walls of Redmires Plantation. Dippers frequent Wyming Brook itself. Common spotted-orchids are beside the lower reservoir and at the start of the path up Wyming Brook (a field opposite is full of them). There are rock water-basins numbered 18-23 along Head Stone Bank (similar to those on Stanage Edge, see *WTP*). Cottongrass grows amidst the heather and cow-wheat among the bilberries.

At The Head Stone. **Inset.** *Male stonechat on a nearby rhododendron (both June 5)*

In the picturesque dell of Wyming Brook (July 28)

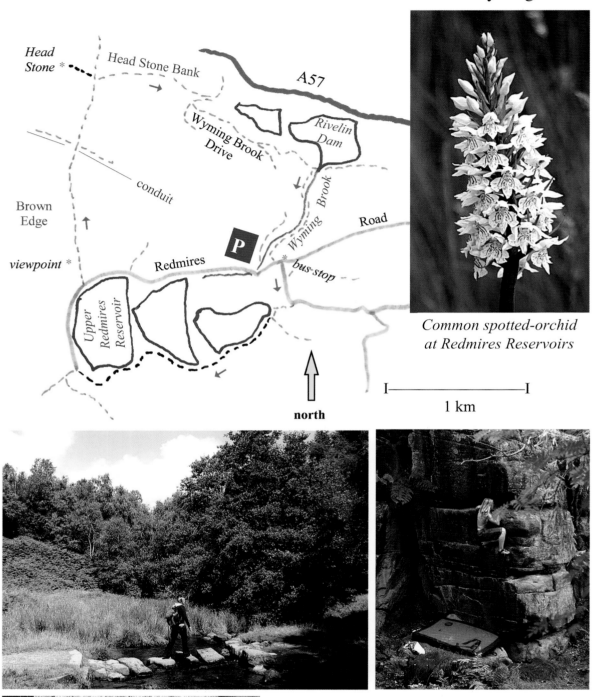

Common spotted-orchid
at Redmires Reservoirs

1 km

north

Above Left. *The stepping stones over Wyming Brook at the start of the walk (July 28).*

Above Right. *A boulderer on the crags beside Wyming Brook.*

Left. *Rock basin No 20 is a good waymark.*

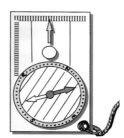

Route From inside the car park walk down to ***Wyming Brook***, cross the stepping stones and walk ahead up steps. Bear right up more steps and keep ahead through stone gateposts to road. Turn left and immediately right up Soughley Lane. Where the lane turns 90° left you turn 90° right through stone stile. After 100m turn 90° left and 30m later turn right through gate to Lower Redmires Reservoir. Follow waterside path which later runs uphill to gate. Bear right. Follow path ahead beside the middle reservoir. About ½ way along, cross boarding on left and walk to left corner of headwall of **Upper Redmires Reservoir**. The path ahead rises then forks. Take right fork. Path later falls to stile and footbridge. Go right over f/b and follow path to wide track, which is the end of **Redmires Road**. Turn right; track becomes a lane. After 500m and just after Remires Plantation car park, go left through gate and on up to another. To visit ***viewpoint***, bear left up to highest hummock. Return to path. One km on, go over bridge across **conduit** and the stile ahead. 500m on there is a junction of paths and a waymark post. Turn left to the ***Head Stone*** and return. Turn right along **Head Stone Bank**. Later the path forks. Take the right fork but to check this is the correct path, walk on 40m and rock basin No 20 should be seen. Return to path which runs down through bracken then ancient pines and birches to track, which is **Wyming Brook Drive**. Turn right. Follow main path until, after ½ km, the path forks at a high, ancient wall on the right. Go left, downhill. After about 400m, in the valley bottom, go through the gate on the right. Take the right fork of the path, uphill. The path soon falls to meander beside Wyming Brook. Ahead, the brook is crossed a few times by footbridges but the path is easy to follow up the dell to reach the stepping stones again and the car park above.

At the bottom of Upper Redmires Reservoir after it was drained in March 2009

23 Whirlowbrook Hall, Porter Valley, Ox Stones and Limb Valley

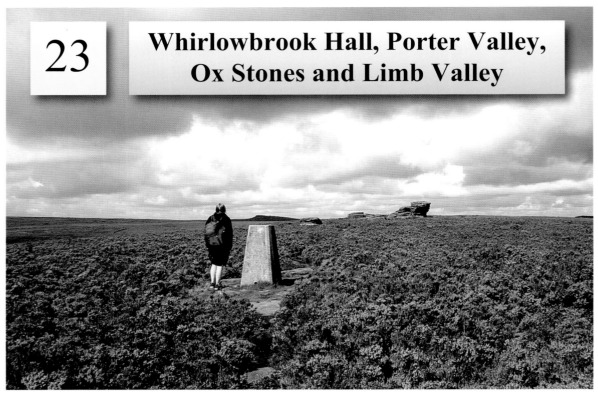

Looking from the trig pillar to the Ox Stones (Aug 13). Stanage Edge is above the pillar.

Starting from Whirlowbrook Hall, the historic valleys of the Limb and Porter are linked by old bridleways, a heather moor and rock features to deliver a walk full of diversity.

Length 12 kms / 7.5 miles **Map** O/S Explorer OL1, *Dark Peak Area*, East Sheet
Start/Finish Whirlowbrook Hall off the A625 at SK 307 828. The grounds of the hall have an upper and lower car park plus conveniences. Buses from Sheffield stop at the start of the walk. Ask for Ecclesall Road South, Whinfell. Traveline : 01709 515 151.
Terrain Easy to follow route on tracks and paths through farmland, woods and moor.
Refreshments Café at Whirlowbrook Hall open summer season weekends. There is a café (chips etc) at Forge Dam open every day of the year. *Norfolk Arms* at Ringinglow.
When To Go/What's There The gardens of Whirlowbrook Hall are a treat throughout the year but are at their best in late spring and summer when the azaleas, rhododendron, ornamental maples, heather garden and formal flower beds glow. The pines see jay, tree creeper, nuthatch and woodpeckers but the lakes have rarely more than mallard, coot and moorhen; but there are damselflies and dragonflies, too. There are conveniences below the hall. Valley woods support bluebell, wood anemone, sanicle, stitchwort, foxglove and wood sorrel. There are brown hares near Ringinglow and a few mountain hares have now extended their range to the heather moors near the *Ox Stones*. Both hares in one walk (if you're lucky!). There are many seats and picnic tables on the walk. There is a toposcope at the head of the Porter Valley aligning near and far landmarks and, if the world was flat, you'd see Chicago 3,836 miles away! Gatekeeper, red admiral, small heath, small copper and green-veined white are among the butterflies. **Nearby** Whirlow Grange occasionally offers outdoor activities including walking (0114 236 3173); Ringinglow Toys sells traditional wooden toys and you can even buy a locally reared alpaca! See sketch map.

Winter in the upper Porter Valley (Jan 29) and ...

... springtime in the beech woods of the Limb Valley (May 10)

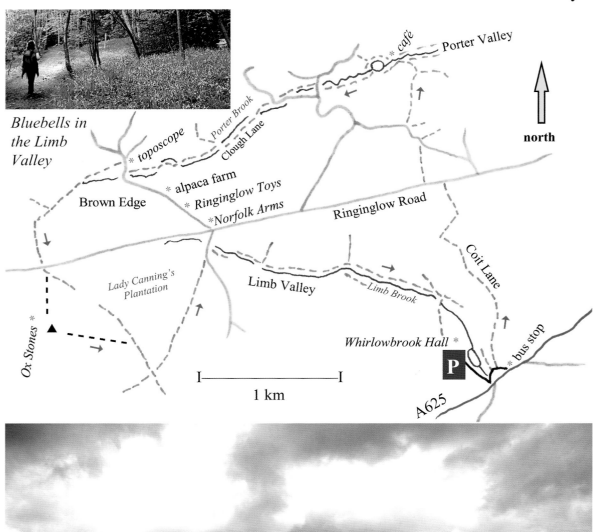

Bluebells in the Limb Valley

At the Ox Stones (Aug 13)

Route Walk down the drive of ***Whirlowbrook Hall*** and out of the entrance gates. Turn left and turn left up the second signposted path on the left. Follow the bridleway (which is **Coit Lane**) until it doglegs down a school drive to **Ringinglow Road**. Cross, turn left then right after 80m down bridleway to road. Cross, turn left (narrow verge); pass two bridleway signs then go over wall stile on the right and walk down the field; over three stiles to stile and track. Turn left then left again at T-junction then bear right at more junctions, passing "Forge Dam" sign on left to enter park. Bear left to the café and go up railed pathway to lake. Turn right. At end of lake, ignore path ahead but bear left to bridge over inflow and follow path to road. Cross. Follow path to lane. Cross and go up path right of **Clough Lane**. It crosses **Porter Brook** and passes a small fall before meeting a track. Cross, and path ahead soon enters woodland. Follow path up beside brook. Cross two footbridges but don't go over a third, but walk ahead up steps to a road. Turn right. At Greenhouse Lane on the right is the *toposcope* and, opposite, a wall stile. Over, follow path ahead then leftish to cross stream (awkward) and stile. Path leads up to access land and stile. Over, bear right then left at fork after 100m and through the heathery quarry hummocks to a road. Cross, then go left through gateposts. After 25m, leave track on right on path which runs south over moor to junction. Turn right to the ***Ox Stones*** then left (115°) to the **trig pillar**. Here, take the left path to meet a track beside woodland. Turn right. At track X-roads turn left down to road. Cross. Turn left then right over stile (info board). After about 100m, bear left to cross the stream and keep left of stream until is passes under small bridge. Here, turn left to triple pathways. Turn right, down steps into woodland. Now follow this path, always ahead, over footbridges and on into mature beech woods. Cross **Limb Brook** on the right over a stone bridge at signposts. Go right at a fork and then left to the upper car park of the hall.

In the formal gardens of Whirlowbrook Hall (May 10)

24 | Oxlow, Eldon Hole, Eldon Hill, Bull Pit, Jackpot (P8) and Rushup Edge

On Rushup Edge with Lose Hill on The Great Ridge in sun ahead (April 25)

A wonderful but fairly tough day out which links ancient lead mine workings; dramatic Eldon Hill Quarries; famous potholes; a wildlife pool and the airy ridge of Rushup Edge.

Length 12 kms / 7.5 miles **Map** O/S Explorer OL1, *Dark Peak Area*, East/West Sheet
Start/Finish Mam Nick car park 3 kms west of Castleton at SK 123 832 (P&D)
Terrain A mix of easy grassy paths; tracks; stony paths and some off-path traverses on Eldon Hill to link the footpaths. It's a steep, uphill off-path climb to gain Rushup Edge.
Refreshments Occasional van in car park otherwise it's Castleton (with Visitor Centre)
When To Go/ What's There A fine outing whatever the season but in May and June wild flowers speckle old mine workings. There's rock-rose, milkwort, mountain pansy, trefoils, hawkweeds, cowslip, mossy saxifrage, early-purple orchid and spring sandwort as well as butterwort and yellow sedge in the limestone flushes. The flowers attract at least nine species of butterfly. The pool beneath Eldon Hill Quarry is maturing rapidly and already attracts emperor, common darter and broad-bodied dragonflies and common blue damselflies. As well as pondweeds, rushes and reeds, kidney vetch, thyme and betony bloom near the water. You pass Windy Knoll Cave which yielded bison, bear, wolf and reindeer remains from an ice age fauna. You also pass Bull Pit, a deep depression now becoming overgrown but once with several pothole aspirations. Nearby, you can (see Route) have a peep at the entrance to the notoriously wet Jackpot (P8) pothole and be thankful you're a walker! One of The Peak's "natural wonders", Eldon Hole is visited. The cavers usually perform at weekends. Apart from the fantastic vista of The Vale of Edale and the Kinder Scout skyline from Rushup Edge, there is a great panorama from the summit of Eldon Hill and also a relict ore-crushing ring (right).

Looking to Mam Tor from "Cook's Cairn" on the summit of Eldon Hill (April 25)

On Rushup Edge, watching them plod up Mam Tor **Inset.** *Emperor dragonfly at the pool*

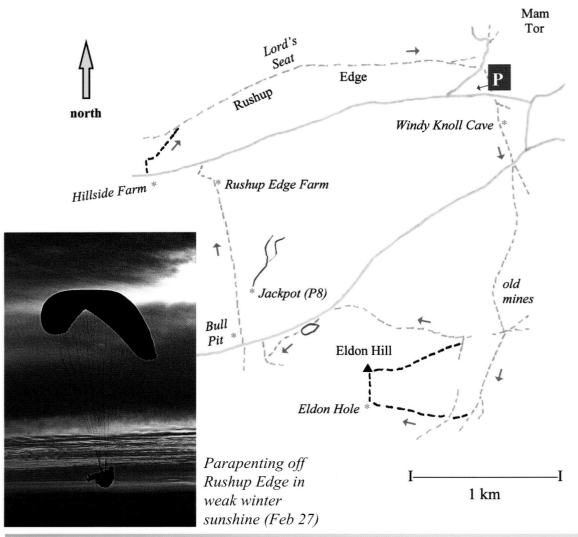

Parapenting off Rushup Edge in weak winter sunshine (Feb 27)

The wildlife pool beneath disused Eldon Hill Quarries (June 25)

Route Turn left out of the car park. After 200m carefully cross road and go through gate. Keep right of rocky **Windy Knoll** to gate and road. Cross. Turn right then left after 10m through gate. After 10m leave track on grassy path ½ right. Path runs up to stile. Over, follow path by wall to stile. Over, follow path down field (mine hummocks to left) to stile and track. Over, turn right go over step-stile or through gate then immediately turn left over stile. Follow grassy path for about 80m where it runs between depressions. Here, take the narrow path left of the left depression. After 100m it crosses a wider path but keep ahead (210°) heading for the middle of a line of trees ahead. At an old wall path joins from right. Go through gap in wall and turn right. Here are a number of paths but bear right through the copse and walk up and follow the wall on the right. Soon it bears left and then you meet a stile complex in the wall. Go over, cross path and head west (284°). Follow animal trail between mine rake on left and rocky escarpment on right. Stay on bearing as escarpment drifts right and head down and up to *Eldon Hole*, which is in a fenced enclosure with trees. Then walk north steeply up to the summit of **Eldon Hill**. From the cairn walk 90° due east and head to old mines encircled by low old walls, where the crushing ring is at the far end. Head on to fence and sheep pen. Turn right and follow fence all way down to wall. Bear left to gate/stile then walk between fence and wall to wall-stile, gate and on to track. Turn left. Follow track, passing Eldon Hill Quarries, all way to road. Turn left. After 80m go over ladder stile on left. Follow right bank of pool, pick up track and follow to fence/stile. Don't go over but turn right to wall stile and road again. Turn left. After 300m, cross road and go through

Having a peep (entirely at your own risk!) into Eldon Hole

gate. Have a peep into *Bull Pit* on left then angle ½ right down long field to stile in fence. (Here, in a depression to your right, a stream disappears down the entrance to *Jackpot* if you want a peep). Over stile, head up long field towards farm and awkward stile in fence. Over, keep ahead, cross watercourse and head up left of another to stile. Over, go through gate that's ahead and on the right into farmyard. Immediately go left through another gate left of the farm buildings and head left then right up steep field to gate (hook behind post) and road. Turn left. Follow left verge for 300m then, just past farm on left, carefully cross road (fast traffic) and go over stile into access land. Head up steep field following wall on right. As it doglegs, go through gap into field on right and head ½ right steeply up to step-stile in wall ahead. Over, turn right. Stay on path left of wall and cross a few stiles on **Rushup Edge**. Near the end of the ridge descend to a wider path on the right which leads to stile/gate and road. Cross road, descend to paved path and turn right to the car park.

Walks On White Peak Map ———————— West Sheet

(Explorer Outdoor Leisure Series No 24)

Beside the Caldon Canal, Leek Branch, in winter (Walk 37, Dec 7)

25 Lamaload Reservoir, Rainow, White Nancy and Ginclough

Lamaload Woods and The Tors (right skyline) from Ely Brow (May 4)

Nestling in the hills to the west of the Goyt Valley, Lamaload Reservoir is a fine starting point for a trip to the Saddle of Kerridge and, the Mecca for all visitors, White Nancy. There are many fine viewpoints and beauty spots on this tough and undulating walk.

Length 13 kms / 8.13 miles **Map** O/S Explorer OL 24, *White Peak Area*, West Sheet
Start/Finish Lamaload Reservoir car park, 5 kms SE of Bollington at SJ 975 753
Terrain Tracks and paths over farmland, muddy after rain. One km of lane at the start.
Refreshments None on route. Detours to pubs at Rainow and Bollington. See O/S map.
When To Go/What's There A walk over the Saddle of Kerridge is not unlike one over the Malvern Hills in that both have Jeckel and Hyde aspects; an industrialised sprawl to one flank and unblemished countryside the other. The Bollington Festival in early May culminates in a torchlight procession up to White Nancy (www.bollingtonfestival.org.uk) Near to Lamaload at SJ 977 759 beside the Bollington road is a memorial stone (below) with an odd tale told on two faces: *Here John Turner was cast away in a heavy snow storm in the night in or about the year 1753* and, *The print of a woman's shoe was found by his side in the snow were (sic) he lay dead.* The fields are home to brown hare, partridge, curlew, skylark and lapwing; and we have seen the odd daytime fox. Redshank and cormorant visit the reservoir along with tufted duck, heron, Canada geese and lesser black-backed gull. The walls have stoats and foxgloves. Buzzards float on high. Mill ruins are met at Rainow. The village has a tower folly and the first recorded dwelling here was dated circa 1150. Three farms were evacuated and drowned to fill Lamaload.

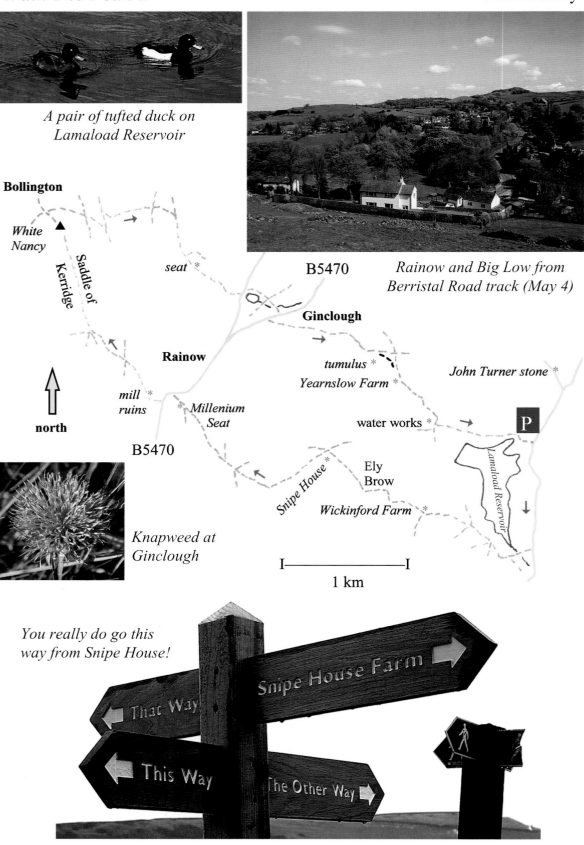

A pair of tufted duck on Lamaload Reservoir

Rainow and Big Low from Berristal Road track (May 4)

Bollington

White Nancy

Saddle of Kerridge

seat *

B5470

Ginclough

tumulus *

John Turner stone *

Rainow

Yearnslow Farm *

mill ruins *

Millenium Seat

water works *

P

north

Ely Brow

Snipe House *

Lamaload Reservoir

B5470

Wickinford Farm *

Knapweed at Ginclough

I———————————I

1 km

You really do go this way from Snipe House!

Snipe House Farm

That Way

This Way

The Other Way

Route Exit the car park and turn right. Follow lane for about a km then turn right through gate on concession path through wood. Descend path; cross stream and rise to meet track. Turn right. Follow track up past footpath No 315 on left to 3-way junction near top of track. Take middle path (½ left) and head for top left of wall on right to gate. Through, keep between fence and wall. Pass through two gates to meet track. Avoid gate ahead. Turn right. Enter yard of *Wickinford Farm*. Go through gate on left. Round paddock to wall step-stile ahead. Cross field to stile in fence. Descend; cross stream and ascend right. Keep on above the dell to wall and fence ahead. Turn left, steeply up **Ely Brow** to gate. On, follow wall on right to wall step-stile and on down through gate to track at *Snipe House*. Turn left. Follow metalled track for 2 kms to meet the **B5470** at **Rainow**. Turn left. Cross road at bus stop; bear left for 50m then turn right down permissive bridleway. Pass mill ruins up to junction. Keep ahead through gateposts to gate. Head up to another gate. Through, take left path up steep, grassy path to wall stile. Over, head up to gate/stile on the **Saddle of Kerridge**. Turn right and pass through 3 kissing gates to reach *White Nancy*. Follow laid path (NW) down to track. Turn right. Follow track down to T-junction. Turn left. After 100m turn sharp right through gate; cross stream; go through gate and on up steps to gate. Keep ahead through 3 more gates to gate and track. Turn right. Follow track up and down to meet lane. Turn left. After 50m go right over stile to wall step-stile right of gate. Follow wall on right to another wall stile. Over, walk ahead for about 50m then descend right to cross stream via stone slab. Over, go **left** to hidden stile/gate. Through, go half-right up to step-stile. Over, bear right up through house drive to B5470 at **Ginclough**. Turn right. After 70m cross road and go up track. Follow it uphill for 1km. It then bends right and there's a viewpoint from the *tumulus* up right. Track falls to pass *Yearnslow Farm* then becomes grassy path down to left of **water works**. Cross stream then turn left uphill (again!). Keep left of track and go through gateposts ahead. Bear right to enter wood via stile. On, follow path to car.

Lamaload Reservoir and its larches in autumn seen from the south (Nov 4)

Monumental White Nancy (July 22). It currently has a black apex ball. During the second world war it was painted green so as not to be an easy landmark for enemy aircraft.

A tough life for livestock on the hills in winter around Lamaload Reservoir (Dec 19)

26 Monk's Dale, Peter Dale, Hay Dale and Wheston Cross

Over the wall step-stile and into Hay Dale (April 11)

These three limestone dales comprise another leg of the Derbyshire Dales National Nature Reserve and are Sites of Special Scientific Interest (SSSIs). From Hay Dale the walk returns via an ancient wayside cross then descends a narrow valley back to Monk's Dale.

Length 12 kms / 7.5 miles **Map** O/S Explorer OL 24, *White Peak Area*, West Sheet
Start/Finish Millers Dale Station car park (P&D) off the B6049 at SK 138 732. There is currently a limited bus service (No 68) which stops outside the car park. It runs from Buxton-Tideswell-Castleton (Traveline 0871 200 2233 : Derbyshire Buses 01298 23098)
Terrain Largely easy to follow paths, tracks and lanes. However, the kilometre through Monk's Dale Wood is very stony and has to be taken with care, as do other rocky paths.
Refreshments The *Angler's Rest* at Miller's Dale.
When To Go/What's There Early February sees a fine snowdrop display at *Curlew Lodge*. Spring; and marsh marigold carpets the wetland in lower Monk's Dale amidst the fool's watercress and water avens. Much more scarce is common butterwort. Violet and wood anemone later bloom under the scrub. May and early June sees the arrival of cowslip, early purple-orchid, kidney vetch and, on a few ledges, Nottingham catchfly - so named as it was first recorded at Nottingham Castle. Mossy and meadow saxifrage, crosswort, rock-rose, thyme and bird cherry are readily observed. The flowers attract common blue, dingy skipper, small copper, orange-tip, northern brown argus and meadow brown butterflies. Birds include green and great spotted woodpecker, grey wagtail, redstart, long-tailed tit, dipper, warblers, buzzard, curlew, wheatear, skylark and kestrel. There are mine relics and a no enter adit in Hay Dale. *Common butterwort at the Monk's Dale flushes*

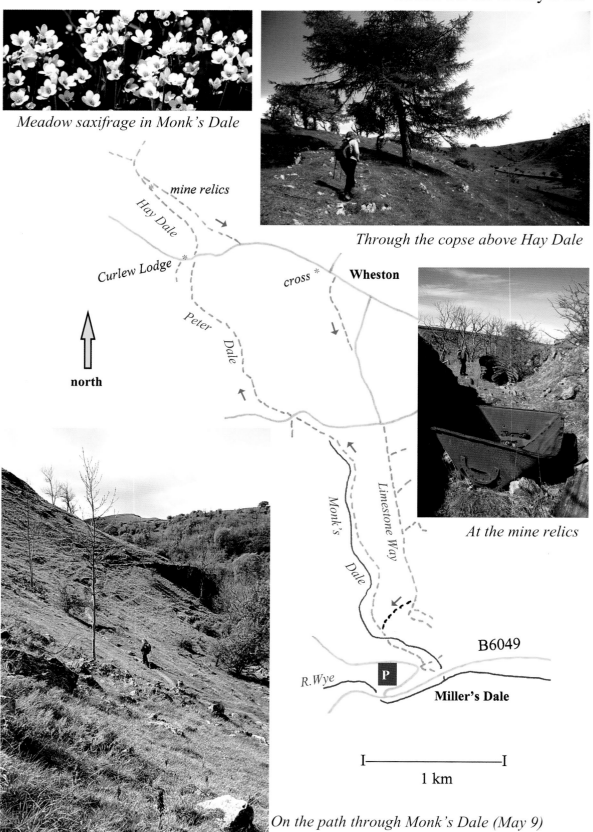

Meadow saxifrage in Monk's Dale

Through the copse above Hay Dale

mine relics

Hay Dale

Curlew Lodge

cross *

Wheston

Peter Dale

↑
north

At the mine relics

Monk's Dale

Limestone Way

B6049

R. Wye

P

Miller's Dale

I————————I
1 km

On the path through Monk's Dale (May 9)

Route Turn left out of car park and walk up the road to where it turns 90° left. Here, go over wall stile on right then through gate ahead. Immediately turn left (left of info board) on path which runs down to footbridge. Cross and bear left on path beside watercourse which leads through trees; passes wetland on left before ***Monk's Dale*** proper appears. Path now forks. Take right path which rises above the valley. Later, this path descends to join the lower path. Keep ahead on valley path which later bears left down a rocky staircase and on to a wall stile at the start of Monk's Dale Wood. Follow the stony path right of the watercourse (which may be dry) for a sustained kilometre obstacle course to a gate. Follow path ahead to road. Cross. Go through wall stile into ***Peter Dale***. Follow path through rocky section; fields; then between crags; always ahead, and on to wall step-stile and road at Dale Head and ***Curlew Lodge***. Turn right. After 30m turn left over stile (keeping left of wall) and walk on to wall step-stile and into ***Hay Dale***. Follow grassy path to gate. Through, after 150m there are ***mine relics*** on the right. Have a look but don't be tempted by the upward slanting path. This is not the exit of the dale which is about 200m beyond. Look out for a narrow path running sharp right from the trees up between small crags. If you go too far and reach stile/gate/info board back-track about 150m to the path. At the top follow it through copse to stile in wall/fence. Over, turn right. Follow wall/fence over long field to wall stile just right of gate. Over, follow track to gate/step-stile. Leave track and go ahead down to wall stile and lane. Turn left to farms and wayside ***cross*** second on the right. Pass junction on left then turn right up track. Follow it to meet farm lane. Keep ahead to T-junction. Cross and go up track. Later, at dogleg, bear right through gate. Path leads to gate. Through, after 30m, turn right through narrow gate. Bear left into narrow valley. Follow path and waymark posts steeply down to waterside path. Turn left; cross f/b and go left on lower path which rises to meet info board in wall. Turn right up to start of walk.

On the path through upper Peter Dale (April 11)

Above. *At the entrance to Peter Dale, but perhaps not today! And that's after negotiating the torrent coming through the gate at the exit to Monk's Dale (**Left**) to get there! These normally dry limestone dales were all flooded during the seemingly endless rainfall in January 2008.*

Below Right. *Top of the weathered wayside cross at Wheston. A gate gains access to the cross, right of Wheston Hall.*

27 Trentabank Reservoir, Macclesfield Forest and Tegg's Nose

On the descent to Hacked Way Lane **Inset.** *Wall butterfly at Tegg's Nose (both Aug 30)*

A fine undulating walk through the woods; over the hills and beside the reservoirs of the Macclesfield Forest. We also visit Tegg's Nose Country Park for the views and heritage.

Length 13 kms / 8.13 miles **Map** O/S Explorer OL 24, *White Peak Area*, West Sheet **Start/Finish** Trentabank Ranger Station and car park (P&D) at SJ 961 711. There are many other free car parks and lay-bys on route (see the O/S map). Buses run from Macclesfield to Langley. This would only add 1 km to the walk : Traveline 08706082608 **Terrain** An easy to follow route on tracks and paths; some are soggy after rain. The walk rises gently up the woods but there are steep bits to Forest Chapel and to Tegg's Nose. **Refreshments** The *Leather's Smithy* pub en route/ weekend snack bar at the car park. **What's There/When to Go** A walk for all seasons. There is a heronry at Trentabank Reservoir, best observed before the leaves come out (end March to end April). The walk passes the observation point with elbow rests for binoculars. In late summer, the formerly quarried outcrop of Tegg's Nose is clad with ling heather. Other plants include heath bedstraw, bell heather, tormentil and mountain pansies. There are quarrying relics and information boards at the site and a toposcope to identify the landmarks. Jodrell Bank radio telescope can be seen on the Cheshire Plain. The woods have wood sorrel, jays, tree creepers, woodpeckers and many fungi in autumn. Waterfowl vary through the seasons but we have seen cormorant, little grebe, great-crested grebe, tufted duck, mandarin duck; as well as coot, mallard and Canada goose. Amphibious bistort is now well-established on two reservoirs and attracts azure and red-eyed damselfly. Buzzard, kestrel and raven are seen in the sky. We have seen eight species of butterfly including speckled wood, wall, small heath and small copper. In late August, Forest Chapel church has a rushbearing ceremony (info 01260 252832). There are many seats for rests on the walk.

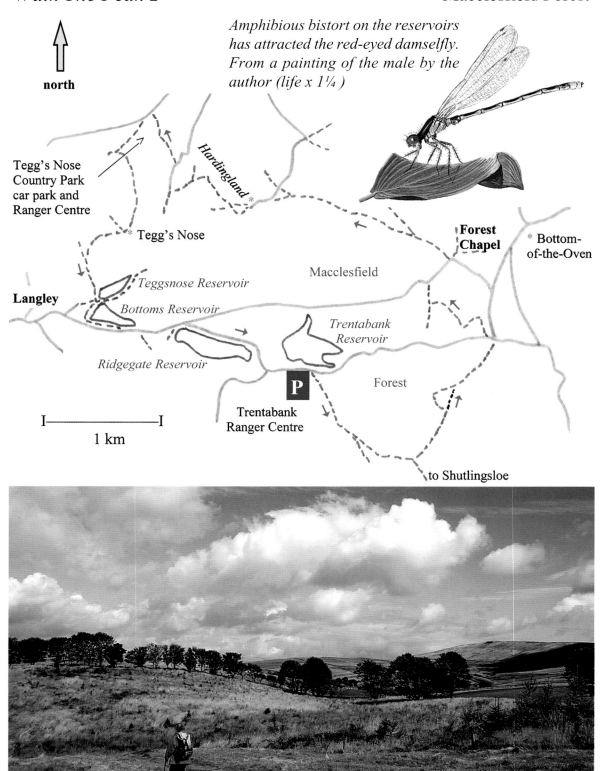

north

Amphibious bistort on the reservoirs has attracted the red-eyed damselfly. From a painting of the male by the author (life x 1¼)

Tegg's Nose Country Park car park and Ranger Centre

Hardingland *

* Tegg's Nose

Forest Chapel

* Bottom-of-the-Oven

Macclesfield

Teggsnose Reservoir

Langley

Bottoms Reservoir

Trentabank Reservoir

Ridgegate Reservoir

Forest

I————————I
1 km

P

Trentabank
Ranger Centre

to Shutlingsloe

On the path from Standing Stone car park, with The Tors right skyline (Aug 30)

Route Walk out of car park, turn right and, after about 200m, turn right up steps (fingerpost to *Wildboarclough*). Through gate, go left (signed *Shutlingsloe*). At fork go right up path; pass heronry viewpoint on left. Path rises to junction. Go ahead (signed *Shutlingsloe*) to another junction and go ahead here, too. Stay on main path until, as it turns 90° left, go ahead up steps. Follow narrow path between trees and on to meet the main track again. Go ahead to gate and road junction. Take road ahead (signed *Forest Chapel*) then turn left into Standing Stone car park. Turn right through gate and head up grassy path which becomes gritted after sign to *Trentabank*. Path enters wood; runs down steps; crosses boarding and runs on to junction. Turn right (signed *Forest Chapel*) up steep path to lane. Turn right. After 250m turn left at cross-ways up *Forest Bridleway* at **Forest Chapel**. Take in views back to Shutlingsloe then, after 300m of the stony track, take the footpath on the left (seat). Follow path through pines, which later becomes mixed woodland. Path falls to X-paths. Go ahead (signed *Tegg's Nose*), left of old barn (*JB 1880*), to junction. Go left (signed *Tegg's Nose*) and on to gate and lane (Hacked Way Lane). Turn left to building (***Hardingland***) ; bear left on track then soon turn right over wall stile. Follow path down field to another stile. Over, turn right down track. Follow stony track all way down. It crosses stream then later becomes a metalled track which finally runs up to a junction. Turn right up lane. After 200m turn left up concession bridleway (*Saddlers Way*). The laid path rises steeply and ends just before the car park at **Tegg's Nose Country**

Park. Walk out of car park; turn left and follow path through gate into the park. After second gate go left up steps and on to junction. Go ahead; pass relics. As path bends to right, a toposcope is at the end of a side path, sharp left. Back on main path, go through gate on left. Keep ahead at bottom of steps where path forks. It later joins a wide, grassy path running downhill to right of wood below. After a kissing gate, path runs steeply down steps. Turn right over headwall of ***Tegsnose Reservoir***. Turn left and immediately right through gate and cross headwall of ***Bottoms Reservoir***. Follow path round and on to opening left of gate. Turn left up road pavement. As it runs out stay on left until it starts again and soon arrives at the *Leather's Smithy* pub at road junction. Go right. Now, there is a choice of following the road beside ***Ridgegate Reservoir*** and bearing left at a junction to ***Trentabank Reservoir*** or, the safer option, taking the specially constructed paths which follow the roads and lead back to the car park.

On the descent from Tegg's Nose (Aug 30)

Tegg's Nose from Bottoms Reservoir (Dec 3)

Shutlingsloe from Saddlers Way   *Some of the quarry relics in the Country Park*

28

Wye Dale, Back Dale, Horseshoe Dale and Deep Dale (north)

Cave-girl contemplations at the entrance of Thirst House Cave

We use an intoxicating aerial view of Wye Dale to link three wildflower limestone dales. Two high level aspects of Topley Pike Quarry put the need for protecting the dales fully into perspective. Fortunately, the Derbyshire Wildlife Trust owns the SSSI of Deep Dale.

Length 12 kms / 7.5 miles **Map** O/S Explorer OL 24, *White Peak Area*, West Sheet
Start/Finish Wye Dale car park opposite Topley Pike Quarry off the A6 at SK 103 725. Trans-Peak buses running between Manchester and Nottingham also stop here.
Terrain Quite a strenuous walk with three steep climbs from the valleys and one very steep descent near the end, where care has to be taken. The A6 has to be crossed twice and a freight rail-line once. Some paths down the dales are very stony. Other paths and tracks are over farmland. Take headlamp to explore Thirst House Cave; watch head!
Refreshments None on route. One km east of the car park, a lay-by often has snack-van.
When To Go/What's There In May, juvenile rabbits scamper amidst the early-purple orchids and cowslips. In July, fragrant and common-spotted orchids mingle with knapweeds, betony, scabious, majoram, harebell, clustered bellflower and hawkweeds above Thirst House Cave; itself having cave spiders and roof engravings, still to be described. In June, Nottingham catchfly and kidney vetch flower on ledges in Deep Dale. You may spot dipper, heron or, rarely, a kingfisher on The Wye. Teasel grows near the remains of a "butter-cross" at King Sterndale. Farmers wives gathered to sell their dairy produce and eggs at such crosses. Pickfords removal company relocated here, too. Burnet rose, herb-Robert, stonecrop and limestone fern grow on scree; thyme and rock-rose on small outcrops. The flowers attract northern brown argus, dark green fritillary, common blue, small copper, peacock and skipper butterflies. Buzzard and kestrel hunt above.

Left. *Nottingham catchfly and kidney vetch in Deep Dale (June 17).*
Right. *The small maze at the junction of Back and Horseshoe Dales.*

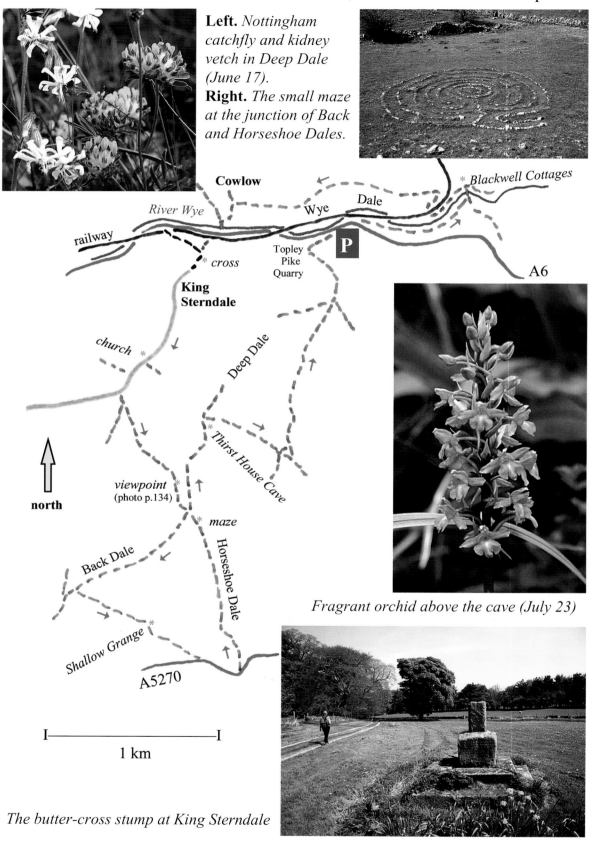

Cowlow

River Wye

Wye Dale

* *Blackwell Cottages*

railway

* *cross*

Topley Pike Quarry

P

A6

King Sterndale

church *

Deep Dale

north

Thirst House Cave

viewpoint
(photo p.134)

* *maze*

Back Dale

Horseshoe Dale

Shallow Grange *

A5270

I———————————————I
1 km

Fragrant orchid above the cave (July 23)

The butter-cross stump at King Sterndale

Route From the CP, walk downstream on the track right of the **River Wye**. Turn left to cross the river at **Blackwell Cottages**. Turn left and the path follows the river before rising right, under a tunnel and on to cross a wooden bridge. The way then rises through scrub to level out at a wood. Follow path left of wall to stile in wall. Cross field to stile at bottom left. Cross next field to stile, again bottom left. Over, descend until wall turns 90° right. Now keep wall on right, always having open land on your left, to meet a stile in a wall/hedge. Over, after 20m turn left on path which spirals down to river. Cross by bridge. Turn right up short roadside path. Carefully cross **A6** and go up path to ladder stile. Carefully cross **railway** line, rise up steps and path to track. Turn left, pass *cross* on left at **King Sterndale**. Follow lane. 250m past church on right, turn left. Go through gate. Leave track and go through 2nd gate. Angle 45° right across field to gate in wall. Repeat this across 2nd field. Turn right through gate; where path forks, go left down path to valley floor. Go through gate, turn immediately right and on to wall stile. Over, ¾ km up **Back Dale** is another wall stile. Don't go over but turn left up to fence stile and wall stile. Over, angle 45° right over field to wall stile; and again to stile in corner of next field. Over to fence stile. Bear left to gate and turn right down drive of *Shallow Grange* to stile left of gateway and ladder stile ahead. Angle right through two fields/stiles to **A5270**. Turn left, stay on verge for 250m then take footpath right of buildings. Two gates lead to **Horseshoe Dale**. Follow dale to stile at entrance to **Deep Dale** and on to *Thirst House Cave* on right. Shortly after cave turn right, steeply up to stile. A few fields/stiles lead to track. Turn left and left again down track which becomes a path. At gate, leave path on right at stile. Over, angle right to stile near pylon. Over, go right down steep path to stile. Ahead, path leads to A6/CP.

Photos July 23

Meadowsweet below the path up from the cave. **Inset.** *Greater knapweed beside the path.*

Burnet rose and herb-Robert flourish on scree in Horseshoe Dale (June 17)

Looking into Deep Dale from the viewpoint (Jan 10)

29

Chelmorton Low, Five Wells, Taddington Moor and Flagg

Rural scene opposite Taddington Moor High Mere (July 2)

An airy walk that visits three high and fairly isolated villages on the limestone plateau. In addition, there are two short detours to optionally see the Neolithic chambered tomb at Five Wells and the twin tumuli on the summit of Chelmorton Low, now on access land.

Length 12 kms / 7.5 miles **Map** O/S Explorer OL 24, *White Peak Area*, West Sheet
Start/Finish There is roadside parking beside Chelmorton church, 1 km SE of the A5270 at SK 115 702. TransPeak buses stop at Taddington; local buses at Chelmorton and Flagg, where the route could be joined (a little extra walking). Traveline 0870 608 2608
Terrain With the exception of the climb up Chelmorton Low and out of Taddington, this is a fairly level walk on paths over farmland. Paths and stiles are slippery after rainfall.
Refreshments Tea rooms at Edge Close Farm, Flagg; *Church Inn* at Chelmorton
When To Go/What's There It's a one km detour to the *Queens Arms* at Taddington if you're gasping by then. In spring, daffodils girdle Flagg and Taddington. Later, curlew and skylark sing on high. Look out for fossils in the wall stiles at the start of the walk. Five Wells Neolithic chambered cairn yielded twelve burials when excavated. Over the years, many stone slabs have been plundered for gateposts and walling. However, its elevated position and atmosphere justify a visit. Chelmorton Low does, too, with fine views from the two Bronze Age summit tumuli. The spring that issues from Chelmorton Low tempted early nomads to settle here on the banks of the stream and the settlement grew from then. The stream has the local name of "Illy Willy Water"! The ancient field systems of Chelmorton are internationally recognised. Flagg Races are held every Easter Tuesday and attract an enthusiastic (and thirsty) throng to the point-to-point scampers. Taddington Moor High Mere has been restored by locals and supports emperor, broad-bodied, southern hawker and common darter dragonflies as well as frogs, newts, great diving-beetles and whirlygig beetles. The vegetation has matured and reed-mace, spike rush and pondweeds are abundant. There are ancient carvings in the porch of Chelmorton church and robins set up house here, too. Brown hares are seen in a number of the fields.

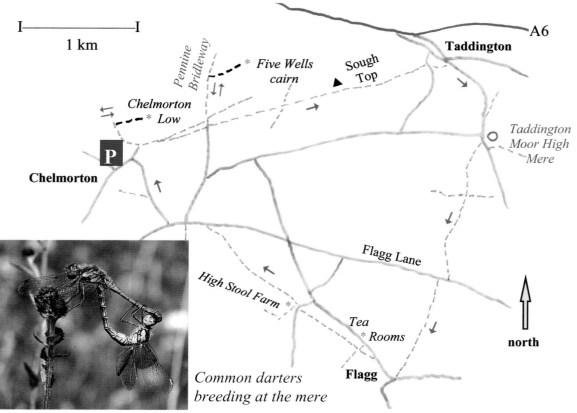

Common darters breeding at the mere

On the path from Flagg to Chelmorton (March 3) **Inset.** *Small tortoiseshell at the mere*

Route At the start of the path left of church, a gate is on the left. To ascend **Chelmorton Low**, go through, bear left and follow path at the bottom of the hill for about 150m then turn 90° right, steeply uphill to the two tumuli on the summit. Return to start. Follow path steadily uphill until it splits. Take left fork to track. To visit *Five Wells* cairn, turn left on the **Pennine Bridleway** for about 300m then right, as directed by fingerpost, on permissive path to barrow. An entrance in a wall gains access. Return to where you joined the PB and take the footpath (via wall steps) to the right of the one to *Five Wells Farm*. Head over the field on the clearly defined path which leads through stiles and fields; crosses a track (Sough Lane); passes the **trig pillar** over a wall on the left and on to the communications mast and reservoir at **Sough Top**. Now angle right to wall stile. Over, bear right, down through wall opening and fields to lane. Cross. Narrow stiles ahead lead on to a wall stile and lane at **Taddington**. Turn right. Follow lane uphill to *Taddington Moor High Mere* on the left (seat, info board). Go through the stile by the road, opposite the mere; cross field to right corner and opening. Cross field to wall stile. Then middle of field to stile right of gate. Cross field bearing right to opening and another, shortly ahead, on the right. Now half-right to stile/ gate. Through and on, rightish, to stile. Over, turn left down long, narrow field to road. Turn right. After 150m, go left onto public footpath (currently diverted and not truly following O/S map). Follow long field to stile on left and on to another stile. Cross to wall stile right of fence. On, keep right of wall to stile. Half way down next field turn left over stile and follow path to road at **Flagg**. Turn right, up Main Road (bus shelter opposite); pass *Millenium Seat* on right then, opposite *Moor View*, go through narrow stile on left to stile at trees and left to another stile. Follow path/stiles ahead to road. Cross, go through narrow gate right of *High Stool Farm*; through gateposts; on to wall stile then through fields/stiles on easy path to follow to road. Turn left and take 2nd right to **Chelmorton**.

Five Wells chambered cairn, viewed from the south (March 3)

Five Wells chambered cairn, viewed from the north (March 3)

Above. *The band of scree on Chelmorton Low came in handy for World Cup fans in 2010! One wonders what our Bronze Age ancestors interred in the tumuli above would have made of it all?*
Left. *After much dedicated restoration work by the local community, Taddington Moor High Mere has matured into a fine wildlife pool (July 2)*

| 30 | **Flash, Wolf Edge, Axe Edge Moor and Brand Top** |

Approaching the trig pillar on Axe Edge Moor (March 4)

A high level hike with fine scenery through the rustic fields and moors south of Buxton. Fairly strenuous, but given an early start and taken at leisure, this is a fine day out.

Length 13 kms / 8.13 miles **Map** O/S Explorer OL 24, *White Peak Area*, West Sheet
Start/Finish A lay-by beside the A53, 9 kms SW of Buxton and just north of the *Travellers Rest* inn at SK 032 678. There is another lay-by further south, and on route, where the road to Flash leaves the A53 at SK 030 674. There is no public transport.
Terrain Paths, tracks and lanes through farmland and over moors. After rain, the final stretch to Dane Head can be very soggy and the trek over Featherbed Moss likewise.
Refreshments *Travellers Rest* inn and *Flash Stores* and *Coffee Shop* at start and finish of walk. The *New Inn* at Flash is also passed (or entered) on route.
When To Go/What's There A walk for all seasons and, when the ground is frozen, the boggy areas are more pleasant to cross. In late summer the heather blooms and the bilberries ripen. Brown hare and the occasional fox appear during the day. The moorland pools support common cottongrass, *Sphagnum* moss, pond skaters and common hawker dragonflies. Wheatear and ring ouzel arrive in summer. Kestrel and peregrine falcon may turn up at anytime. One meadow blossoms with harebell, hawkweeds, eyebright and tormentil. Other flora seen on the way are foxglove, rose bay and great willowherb, gorse, meadow vetchling, herb-Robert, deergrass, yarrow, hard fern, knapweed, ragwort, lungwort, umbellifers, fodder vetch, greater bird's-foot trefoil, creeping and spear thistle. Small white is the most abundant butterfly; others include small heath, meadow brown, comma, small skipper and small tortoiseshell. There is a fine 360° panorama from the trig pillar with many old friends being seen from unusual aspects: Thorpe Cloud, Mam Tor, Kinder Scout, High Wheeldon, Chrome Hill, The Roaches and Minning Low (with bins).

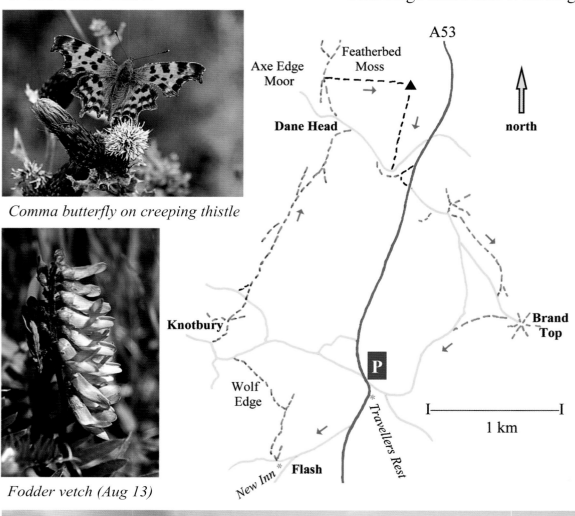

Comma butterfly on creeping thistle

Fodder vetch (Aug 13)

Looking to The Roaches from the track to Wolf Edge (Aug 13)

Route From the lay-by, walk south down the **A53** on the pavement on the east side of the road. After 400m, carefully cross the road and turn up the minor road signed to *Gradbach Youth Hostel*. The road forks in the village of **Flash**, so take the right fork and pass the *New Inn*. About 200m after, turn right then bear left to pass *Far View Cottage* to stile/gate. Don't take footpath right, but walk down track, keeping right at what seems a fork to a stile/gate and on up to waymark post. Turn left over stile right of gate and head up walled path to breach **Wolf Edge**. Path leads down to stile. Over, follow fence to stile on right. Over, bear left and down over clapper bridge to lane. Turn left then right at a junction. After 200m, turn right and stay on track to ladder stile on right. Over, go ahead, just left of old wall to reach gate and lane. Turn left, keep ahead at junction and stay on track until it turns sharp left. Here, go ahead through gate and up wide path. Pass path off left to gate and on over the moor to reach a lane at **Dane Head**. Turn left then right onto path after 200m. Pass *pool* on right to join track. Bear right. Track levels over **Axe Edge Moor** and, as it swings left, leave it on faint path left of fencing. Path runs east down then up **Featherbed Moss** to trig pillar. Here, turn right on path that runs south for about 1 km to reach lane. Turn right and, after 100m, turn left down footpath to stile at old lay-by. Bear right to A53. Cross and go down road signed to *Brandside*. As road turns sharp right, leave it on track ahead (not f/p left). Follow track to building then the path left of it to gate. Ahead, pass isolated stone gateposts on left (photo) to stile left of building at entrance to a wood. Walk up "drive" of *Bird Farm* to stile/gate and on up to lane. Turn left. Ignore path left (down to Brandside Farm) but walk on lane to dwelling at **Brand Top**. About 75m on, turn sharp right and walk down track which runs pleasantly down to a lane. Keep ahead, down the lane which crosses a brook and then finally rises quite steeply to join a road. Turn right to the lay-by and the refreshments on offer at the *Flash Stores* and *Coffee Shop* or the **Travellers Rest**.

Chrome Hill (centre, left) peeps into view from the path to Brand Top (Aug 13)

On the descent from Wolf Edge towards Knotbury, with Shutlingsloe, left (Aug 13)

Looking left to Thirkelow Rocks from the path over Brand Side (March 4)

31 Pot Lords, Greasley Hollow, Wincle Minn and Croker Hill

Looking back on the route taken to Mareknowles on a drizzly autumn day (Oct 19)

This day-long ramble begins through farmland and rises to Pot Lords and the Hanging Gate before visiting the atypical stone "circle" of The Bullstones. A fall to the atmospheric and wooded Greasley Hollow is followed by a trek along the spine of the region.

Length 14 kms / 8.75 miles **Map** O/S Explorer OL 24, *White Peak Area*, West Sheet
Start/Finish Roadside parking on the west side of Hollin Lane opposite *Lower House Farm*, itself 400m NW of the *Ryles Arms* at SJ 938 696. There is no public transport.
Terrain Tracks and paths through farmland, some of which are not often walked and may be indistinct. Greasley Hollow is usually tacky. The A54 has to be crossed twice.
Refreshments The *Hanging Gate*; The *Wild Boar* and The *Ryles Arms* may be open.
When To Go/What's There A walk for all seasons but go after a few dry days. Every other Sunday morning between July and February the Wild Boar Clay Pigeon Club shoot near the route, but signs are erected and their lookouts will halt proceedings and escort you safely through (honestly). Wincle's *Millennium Stone* is passed and was erected by the local WI ("And did those feet..."). The *Bullstones* is now classified as the last remaining stone circle in Cheshire, but its origins and builders may have been from the west, perhaps Wales. The footbridge in Greasley Hollow was erected by the *Peak & Northern Footpaths Society*. (If you wish to join them visit www.peakandnorthern.org.uk). Birds include snipe, partridge, skylark, green and lesser spotted woodpecker, redstart and treecreeper. Rabbits and hares flee stoat and fox on the ground, but buzzard, goshawk and raven are ready for the exhausted stragglers. Plants include harebell, cuckooflower, foxglove, yarrow, wood sorrel and hawkweeds.

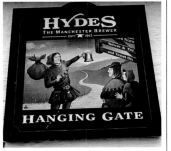

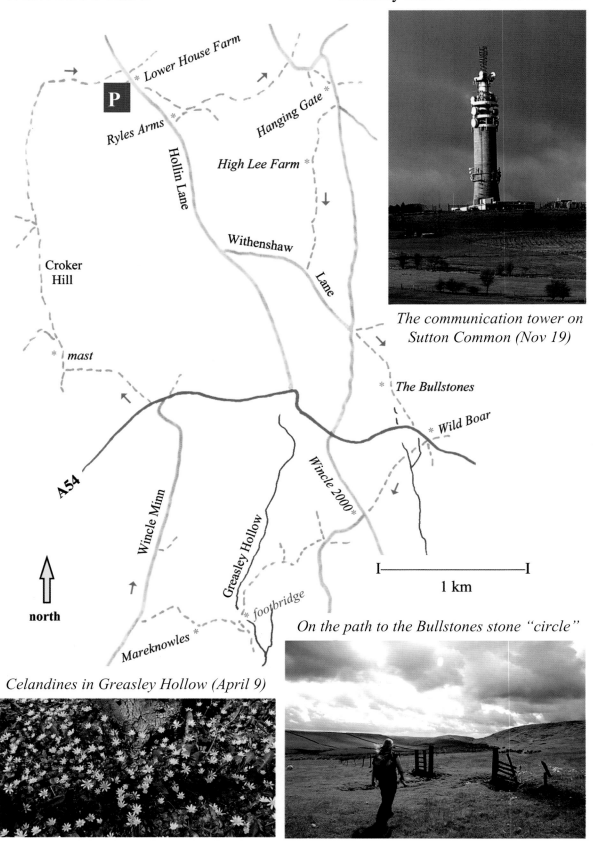

The communication tower on Sutton Common (Nov 19)

On the path to the Bullstones stone "circle"

Celandines in Greasley Hollow (April 9)

Route From the parking area walk SE a little. On left is *Lower House Farm*. Pass it and go through gate on left up to another gate. Follow field just right of trees to gate. Bear right down to gate and lane. Turn left (not ahead) then right on permissive path beside stream to gate and field. Head up to gate then bear right on path right of hedge and along "crest" to gate. Through, bear right, left of wall; through gate to track, gates and road. Turn right up road. After 200m, turn right up second footpath; up steps and through gate to **Hanging Gate** pub. Turn right on road. After 150m, turn right over stile and walk half left down to bottom right corner of field. Follow path left of wall to stile and on through waymarked field then down to footbridge. Go over stile; bear left and rise above stream. Keep just left of fence to stile. Bear right to stile left of **High Lee Farm**. Bear left up track; through gateposts ahead (not left) and cross field to stile left of trees and lane. Turn left up **Withenshaw Lane** to T-junction. Cross road and go over the right of two stiles to another stile/gate. After another stile, head half right up field to **Bullstones** "circle" then return to path. It rounds hill to gate and then stiles and gate through farmyard to **A54**. Turn left. At **Wild Boar Inn** cross road. Go over stile right of gates. Walk just right of wall then fence down to stile. Over, head half-right up field to ladder stile in wall, half way up field. Then angle up to top left of next field (fine view behind) to stile and road. Cross. Go down lane ahead. After about 300m, at junction, go ahead down track (cattle grid/stile) then over another cattle grid/stile. As track veers right to farm, go ahead over stile and through gate. Keep right of hedge as it swings left down to stile and footbridge. Over, keep ahead to stile and on to waymark post. Turn right up to ruins of **Mareknowles** and track. Pass cool house on right and walk to top of hill via gate to lane. Turn right. Follow lane over **Wincle Minn** and down to A54 again. Turn left. Stay on left verge until safe to cross road (150m?) then go down track. After 300m, leave track on left and walk up fields with stiles to left of Sutton Communications **mast** and lane. Turn right. 80m past mast take second track on right to stile/gates. Keep ahead right of wall down long field to gate. Through, keep left of wall to gate, then through a second and a third gate. Through, head to wall on right. Keep left of it to gate. Bear left then right to stile and down to another. Over, head down field (waymark post) to track, a stile and then a permissive path down to a road and your car.

Some of the ruins at Mareknowles (Oct 19)

The footbridge in Greasley Hollow (Oct 19)

At the Bullstones stone circle before a storm (July 30)

32 Swallow Moss, Upper Elkstone, Brownlow Bridge and Revidge

Approaching the trig pillar, cairn (and squall) at Revidge (Aug 12)

A wild walk on ways seldom trod and well-away from the hotspots. The nature reserve of Swallow Moss is crossed en route to an expansive view before Upper Elkstone. From here a high level traverse leads down to Brownlow Bridge and on to the moors of Revidge.

Length 12 kms / 7.5 miles **Map** O/S Explorer OL 24, *White Peak Area*, West Sheet **Start/Finish** Room for a few cars at the end of the lane that leads from opposite Shawfields Farm to Cuckoostones and Revidge Wood at SK 078 604. If full, there is ample roadside parking on the lanes through Swallow Moss. There is no public transport. **Terrain** A real mix of paths and tracks over moor, rough pasture and farmland. A few lanes, too. Route finding is tricky in places so map-reading skills would be beneficial. **Refreshments** None on route, but nearby Warslow often has a beer festival 1st Sat July! **When To Go/What's There** A walk for all seasons but hard after snow. Swallow Moss has a good population of adders (and lizards for them to eat) but keep to the paths and you'll be OK. The roadside ditches beside the moss have marsh valerian, sneezewort, devil's bit scabious and, rather strangely, lily-of-the-valley. Other wetland plants include woodruff, cuckooflower, marsh marigold and butterbur. The moss and moors support deergrass, meadow fox-tail, cross-leaved heath, stunted gorse, ling heather, hare's tail and common cottongrass. In spring you pass primrose, violet, red campion, bluebell, greater stitchwort and blackthorn. Later, knapweed, hawkweeds and yellow loosestrife bloom. Brown hare and weasel may appear. Skylark and curlew call from aloft and warblers sing to each other and us as well. Currently, there is an unusual "cairn" beside the trig pillar at Revidge. Probably a pet memorial, but who knows? Someone does! Is it you? Email me: roddunn@hotmail.co.uk *Sneezewort*

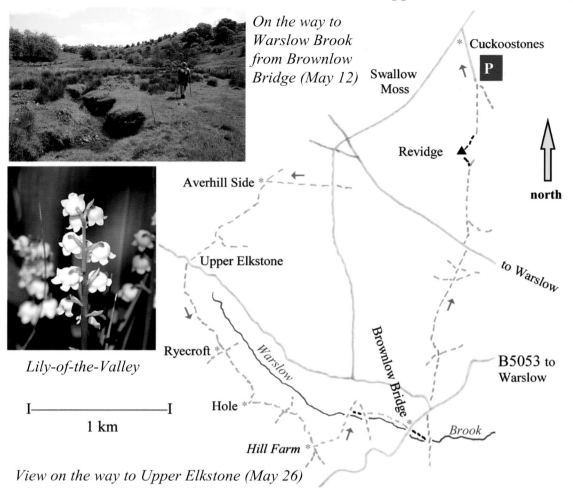

On the way to Warslow Brook from Brownlow Bridge (May 12)

Lily-of-the-Valley

Cuckoostones

Swallow Moss

Revidge

north

Averhill Side *

Upper Elkstone

to Warslow

Ryecroft *

Warslow

Brownlow Bridge

B5053 to Warslow

Hole *

Brook

Hill Farm *

I————————I
1 km

View on the way to Upper Elkstone (May 26)

Route From the parking spot, walk back down the lane to the junction. Turn left. Follow the lane through **Swallow Moss** for 1¼ kms to X-roads. Walk ahead to another X-road. Also go ahead. After 250m, turn right through gate. Follow path left of wall to boarding and stile in wall. Over, cross field to another stile and then another into the farmyard at **Averhill Side**. Walk through the farm to metal gate just ahead. Through, immediately turn left and walk down very long field, keeping right of fence and following it as it falls to the wooded valley bottom and a footbridge. Cross. Pass through gate to footbridge. Here, bear right over stile to another footbridge. Cross and head up field to gate at top left of field and on to road at **Upper Elkstone**. Turn left, cross road and go up Church Lane. Pass *Furlong Farm* to end of track then go over stile on right and bear left down field to footbridge. Over, follow fence to farm at **Ryecroft**. Ahead, follow waymark signs through the trees to stile and on to footbridge. Over, keep right of fence through long field to gate. Bear right to gate left of building. Follow path round **Hole Farm** to track. Bear left. After 50m go right through gate and follow path to another gate. Ahead, follow hillside path round stream then bear right up narrow path (sign) to stile/gate at *Hill Farm*. Go between buildings to gate/stile then turn sharp left to stile and ahead to another. Keep right of hedge/fence to stile. Over, head straight downhill (aiming for farm across the valley) to footbridge. Over, turn right and follow *Warslow Brook* and stiles to **Brownlow Bridge**. Cross **B5053**, go over stile and follow fence to footbridge. Don't cross but turn 90° left up field to B5053 again. Very carefully cross road; turn right then left (signed *Elkstone*). After 30m, go over stile on right and follow path to stile and on up long field to wall step-stile. Keep left of barn to wall stile ahead. Over, and on to wall stile. Over, pass gate on left to gate ahead. Head up track for 400m. As it turns right, go through stile on left; turn right and follow wall on right up to top of field; gate/stile and road. Turn left. After 25m cross and go over stile. Keep left of wall then, near top of field, angle left to squeezer-stile at wooden gate. Over, follow path right of wall to stile on left. Over, bear right up path left of fence to start of pine wood and pole across track. Here, turn left off track onto narrow path and on to junction. Bear left to trig pillar on **Revidge**. Return to junction; bear left and follow path until it rejoins the main track. Keep ahead on the track back to the car parking area.

Approaching Revidge on the path from Brownlow Bridge (Jan 17)

A wild day on the track from Revidge back to Cuckoostones (Aug 12)

On the path over the moor to Averhill Side (May 26)

From left to right : Hen Cloud, The Roaches, Ramshaw Rocks and Shutlingsloe seen from the footpath near to the Mermaid Inn (Nov 22). Jodrell Bank peeps above Hen Cloud.

This wild, airy walk through the eastern Staffordshire Moorlands reveals some outstanding, open panoramas and also some secluded, tranquil hideaways. But be warned; this is The Peak District in the raw and many footpaths are seldom trodden.

Length 12 kms / 7.5 miles **Map** O/S Explorer OL 24, *White Peak Area*, West Sheet
Start/Finish Off-road parking for about 10 cars on the west side of the minor road just south of the trig pillar on Hill House at SK 050 584. If full, there is a small lay-by for about 4 cars opposite Blake Mere at Merryton Low at SK 040 612. The route passes here.
Terrain Largely moorland paths, some of which are indistinct so take binoculars to spot the stiles. There is an off-path kilometre over similar ground. A stream has to be crossed. There is a small, permanently wet marsh which has to be negotiated to reach a footbridge over Warslow Brook. Some of the farms are basic, and passage through them yukky.
Refreshments The walk passes the *Mermaid Inn*, but it is not always open.
When To Go/What's There In late summer the heather adds its beauty, but the autumn browns and golds are equally attractive. Path-following is tricky so not advisable after snow. There is a stream to cross and some marshy areas, so go after some dry weather. The parking area is also used by model aeroplane clubs so you could spend a few minutes watching the aerobatics, but beware of low flying aircraft! The farmland and moorland supports brown hare, skylark, lapwing, curlew and fox. Snipe are flushed from some marshy patches. A cuckoo is occasionally heard and a ring ouzel seen. There are ravens, kestrels and peregrines have bred at The Roaches and hunt overhead. Blake Mere has cotton-grass, common hawker, black darter and four-spot chaser dragonflies. We have disturbed herons here, twice. In spring there are wild primroses, violets and bluebells near Herbage. Flushes have marsh marigold, cuckooflower and water-crowfoot.

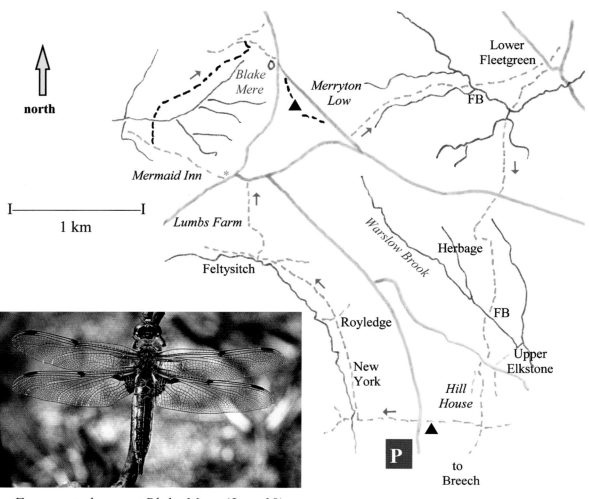

Four-spot chaser at Blake Mere (June 10)

At a windswept Blake Mere. The walker is centre, far bank (Oct 24). See also p.244

Route Go through the stile on the opposite side of the road to the **trig pillar** and walk west down the field, track and field again to the valley bottom. Turn right, keep right of the cattle grid, and head over the long field, aiming for the middle of the wall ahead, where there is a loose stile. More fields and stiles (passing **New York** on the way!) then keep left of **Royledge Farm** to a stile near the corner of walls up ahead. Over, keep right of wall to stile then cross the farm track and head to right of building ahead. A stile leads to another in a wall. Now angle left down to the farm at **Feltysitch**, where a watercourse has to be crossed and the farmyard passed through before you can bear right over marshy ground to a fence and trees. Keep just left of fence to stile at pylon. Over this, another leads you to the track to **Lumbs Farm** and on to a road. Turn left to another road, over which is the **Mermaid Inn**. Go through the gate left of the car park and stay close to the track until a stile and signposts are met. Over, walk downhill, off path, and at 90° to the valley on the right. Here, carefully cross the stream at an appropriate place and walk uphill for about 100 metres or so to a ridge, where The Roaches come in to view again. Turn right along the crest and follow it to the head of the valley, where a fence is met. Turn left and follow the fence to a stile after about 100 metres. Over, follow the tyre ruts as they angle right to join a track, with **Blake Mere** down to the right (seat). Cross the road and take the left minor road. After a few metres, go up the path to the trig pillar at **Merryton Low**. Then turn left on a path back to the road. Follow for 300 metres and turn left on to the moor, keeping left of a watercourse. Pass orienteering post DH on the way to stile at fence. Over, follow the embankment; it bears right, then pass ruin and keep ahead down to a **footbridge** at an enchanting location. Head uphill from the FB to a ladder stile, another FB and then on to a gate, right of buildings. Pass through farmyard at **Lower Fleetgreen** and down the farm track, which is left to a stile. The way leads over more fields and stiles then runs through heather to a road. Turn right and right again after 40 metres. Keep left as track forks down to stream (FB and "bridge"). Cross, right is orienteering post DO, keep left of it between watercourses and head up just right of the farm and go through gap in fence opposite farm and up to gate and on to road. Cross, keep right of ancient hawthorns and down to boggy area and up to farm track. Turn left, pass between buildings at **Herbage** and, as track peters out, bear right, downhill keeping left of watercourse and through a very marshy stretch to a **footbridge**. Onwards the way leads leftish uphill through two gates and Manor Farm to a road at **Upper Elkstone**. Turn right and after 70 metres turn left up Well Lane. Keep left as track forks. Stay on track until just before a farm, turn right, go over two stiles and walk steeply uphill to the trig pillar and the road. Turn left to parking area.

Watching members of the Leek and Moorlands Model Aeroplane Club perform near to the trig pillar at Hill House.

Top. *Down the moor from Merryton Low to orienteering post DH and on to Lower Fleetgreen (Aug 28)*

Above Left. *Passing the Millennium Beacon on the footpath beside the Mermaid Inn (Nov 22)*

Above Middle. *At the trig pillar on Merryton Low. Here there is a Roll of Honour to the 5th Staffs Leek Battalion Home Guard, 'C' Company. There is also a fine panoramic view*

Above Right. *The footbridge over the head of Warslow Brook. Before the FB, a marshy area has to be negotiated (May 8)*

Left. *The artistic pub sign at the Mermaid Inn*

34 | Wetton Mill, Waterslacks, Swainsley, Ecton Hill and Sugarloaf

Looking to Sugarloaf (left) and the Wetton Hills from the path above Hoo Brook (May 1)

This short but most engrossing walk begins by Hoo Brook before rising to a fine view of jagged Sugarloaf. A unique Peak road tunnel is passed en route to a wonderful folly and a steep pull up to ancient copper mines and onwards to Ecton Hill summit and the views.

Length 9 kms / 5.63 miles **Map** O/S Explorer OL 24, *White Peak Area*, West Sheet
Start/Finish Car parks beside the *Manifold Way* at Wetton Mill SK 094 561.
Terrain Easy to follow route with a very steep (but mercifully short) climb up to Ecton Hill from the Manifold Valley. The path beside Hoo Brook becomes very tacky after rain and the descent beneath Sugarloaf is steep and stony. But, taken steadily, it's a fine walk.
Refreshments There is a café at Wetton Mill, most often open in summer.
When To Go/What's There Originally owned by the Duke of Devonshire, the copper and some of the profit from the mines at Ecton were funnelled into a number of projects including most of the fine buildings in Buxton, including the fabulous Opera House (see a show!). En route, the spire of the folly is coppered green from the said mines; another example being the spire of Sheen church (seen from Walk 32). The mineshafts are now much more protected for us walkers than they used to be but provide stiff challenges for underground explorers. The only road tunnel in The Peak can be entered on the way. The bird song in the valley when the migrant songbirds join the symphony of the residents is mesmeric in April and May. Gorse clads the flanks of the valley and flowers at any time, including Christmas! In early summer, the aromatic almond essence scent of the these flowers intoxicate and entice birds, butterflies, bugs and other insects to the plants. Linnets and goldfinches nest here and small ermine moth larvae weave their protective spider-like webs over hawthorn as well.   *Mountain pansies on Ecton Hill*

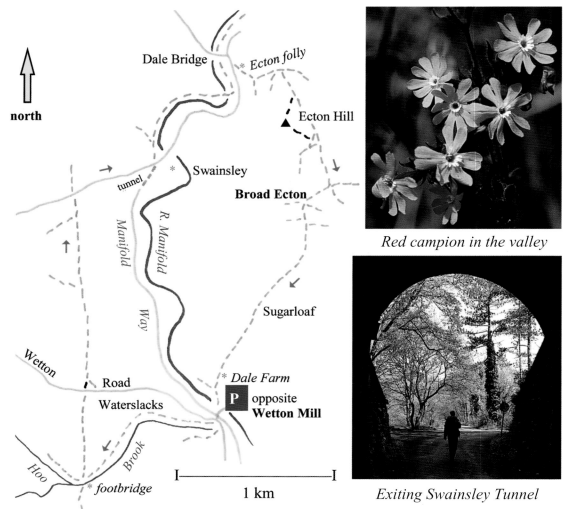

Red campion in the valley

Exiting Swainsley Tunnel

Checking out the landmarks from the summit of Ecton Hill

Route Go to the X-roads and turn right (signed *Butterton*). Leave the road after 50m and go through gate on left. Ahead is a gate/stile and after the path follows **Hoo Brook** through **Waterslacks** to a gate (or stile) and on to a footbridge. Don't cross but turn 90° right uphill, right of a hedge. As you near the top there are views to the right. You meet a gate and ahead walk up the track to a stile and **Wetton Road**. Cross, go over stile and field to gate. Ahead, keep left of dwelling and proceed down field to gate/stile and on to twin gates; then angle left to gate in wall. Path ahead leads half-left down field to cross stream. After the gate, follow path left of hedge to gate/stile and on to a gate and farm track, which is followed to a road. Turn right and follow road to valley floor and a junction. Turn left (signed *Manifold Valley* and *Wetton Mill*). Our route then turns right, but to have a peep at the tunnel turn left and return. Follow the **Manifold Way** for about a km; cross the **River Manifold** and head to a gate. Turn right then right at road T-junction then left after 15m up track (signed *Top of Ecton*). Pass through the arch of the folly at **Ecton** and take path left of gate to wall-steps. Over, go ahead uphill (not path right), very steeply at first but path then winds up less painfully to mine buildings, where you turn 90° right at wall. Walk left of mineshafts (now fenced off) up to gate. Bear right on concession path to trig pillar on **Ecton Hill** and then turn left passing more mine shafts to rejoin public footpath at stile and 5-way finger post. Turn right through gate (signed **Broad Ecton**) and walk down field to stile and keep ahead to track. Turn left and follow track until, at left bend, gates on right lead to path left of wall and on to gate. Onwards, keep ahead through opening and keep left beside wall as a track branches right and go down to wall stile and NT sign (*Dale Farm*). Through, go over stile on left (with *Access Land* sign and gate). There follows a short but steep and stony downhill section to the valley. Keep left at track hairpin; go over stile at, and pass through **Dale Farm**. Follow the track ahead to **Wetton Mill** and car park over the bridge.

Looking down on the gorse-clad Manifold Valley from the way to Ecton Hill (May 1)

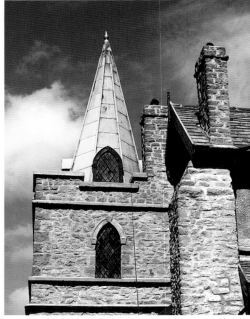

Top Left. *Copper mineshaft with cavers' iron anchor point and smelting house on Ecton Hill.*
Above. *The copper spire on the folly at Ecton, made from the ore mined here.*
Below. *A fine example of geological rock folding beneath Apes Tor.*

35

Grindon, Ford, Onecote and Butterton

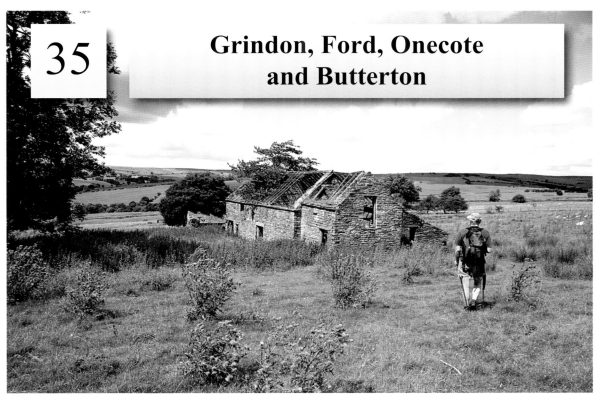

Farm ruins and spear thistle on the way to Grindon Moor (July 23)

This excursion to four fairly remote rural communities on the high limestone plateau starts at Grindon with its unusual Rindle Stone; descends to the hamlet of Ford; meanders to Onecote; ascends to cross Grindon Moor then crosses ancient fields to Butterton.

Length 12 kms / 7.5 miles **Map** O/S Explorer OL 24, *White Peak Area*, West Sheet
Start/Finish Car park near Grindon church at SK 084 545. There is no public transport.
Terrain Predominantly paths over livestock farmland together with a little rough heath.
Refreshments *Jervis Arms* at Onecote; *Black Lion* at Butterton (built 1782)
When To Go/What's There A bracing outing whatever the season but go after a few dry days. In summer, curlew and skylark call above the rough pastures. Grindon Moor is a small remnant of the limestone heath that once covered much of this upland before being "improved" to grazing pasture. The drains around the moor support devil's-bit scabious, spearwort, knapweed and sneezewort. Other plants seen on the walk include tormentil, hawkweeds, pink parslane, foxglove, clovers, marsh marigold and rose bay willowherb. Amongst the heather, stunted gorse, cross-leaved heath and cottongrass bloom. Brown hare, fox, partridge and wheatear may appear. A rindle is a stream running only after rainfall. The stone announces the claiming of this water by a mean old git (see info board in CP). Grindon Moor also holds a sad story: On 13th February 1947 a Handley Page Halifax bomber RT922 of 47 Squadron of the RAF crashed here killing the six crew and two press photographers. The plane was on a mercy mission dropping supplies to these villages; snow-bound and cut-off after weeks of snow. Newspaper reports, photos and letters are in Grindon church and there is a memorial cairn on a footpath at SK 06340 55296. Access via Quarry Farm (see sketch map).

Devil's-bit scabious

The road ford at Butterton (June 12) **Inset.** *The Cavalier Inn is now a private residence*

Route Turn left out of car park and follow wall on left to the Rindle Stone. Walk up road leading to church; keep left at junction and left again at another. After 100m, turn right over obscured stile just right of the old *Cavalier Inn*. Go up middle of field to wall step-stile. Over, stay just right of fence to stile. Over, ahead to ditch and gate. Through, go ahead on path then left to gate, left of trees. Through, turn right to gate then follow fence over long field to stile in field corner. Over, follow fence to stile in the fence, right of gate. Over, bear ½ left to stile in fence. Over, go ½ right, bisect track to stile in fence corner. Over, go ½ right, cross track and head to left of farm and stile (fingerpost). Over, turn right to wall step-stile. Over, go to track but soon leave it at left bend and head ½ right up field to step-stile in field corner and road. Cross, go over stile and head ½ right to stile in hedge and road. Turn left and walk down to hamlet of **Ford**. At the bridge over the *River Hamps*, don't go over but bear right then left, keeping left of building and then between buildings on path to stile. Over, bear left and go up track which later joins another. Turn right. Later track swings right. Here, walk ahead to stile. Over, head down left a little then go ahead and cross ditch by tractor crossing then ahead to gate/stile. Keep ahead over next long field to waymark post near pylon. Keep right of the line of pylons to another waymark post a little up to the right then go ahead to another waymark post at an electric fence and on to wall stile. Over, keep ahead to stile and road at **Onecote**. Turn right (or left to *Jervis Arms*). Stay on right verge. After 150m pass FP sign on right and, 80m on, turn right up lane. After 400m leave track at right bend and go over stile on left. Keep left of pylons to top pylon and on to NT sign and stile. Over, follow path over **Grindon Moor** to road. Cross. Go over stile to track. As it bends right keep ahead to stile and on through gate and ahead down field to left of ruin. Cross stream and go

over two stiles to farm. Keep right of it to stile. Over, follow the easy-to-see path through 8 narrow fields (stiles and gates) to a wall corner. Here, keep ahead left of wall to stile in this wall. Follow path down to steps, gate and the cobbled ford at **Butterton**. Turn right (or left and right at fork uphill to *Black Lion*). Stay on uphill road for ½ km then go through gate on left. Turn right and soon go over boards to gate. On, go ahead to gate and on by hedge to gate. Keep ahead to another gate. Over, go ½ right to stile. Over, go ahead, cross track and enter farmyard at *Hillsdale*. Turn left to metal barred gate. Through, turn right to stile hidden in hedge below. Over, go ahead up field to stile in fence between tall trees. Over, go ½ right up to waymark post and on to stile in fence over ditch. Over, follow fence on right to very narrow squeezer-stile. Through, walk on and through another, and keep left of the hedge over a long field to a stile and the car park at **Grindon**.

Reading the Rindle Stone, Grindon

Top. *The path touches the upper reaches of the River Hamps.* **Middle.** *The small but precious tract of limestone heath on Grindon Moor.* **Left.** *Pink parslane at Ford.* **Above.** *The memorial cairn to 47 Squadron.*

36

The Highest Wetton Hill, Narrowdale Hill and Gratton Hill

Narrowdale Hill (Aug 27). The ascent initially follows the wall in the centre of the shot.

From many aspects the undulating and tempting hills around Wetton beckon the walker. Access land agreements now permit three of the main hills to be gained in a single walk. Nearby Wolfscote Hill (see page 228), is an additional recommended top.

Length 11 kms / 6.88 miles **Map** O/S Explorer OL 24, *White Peak Area*, West Sheet
Start/Finish Wetton village car park (with PCs, nearby campsite) at SK 109 551
Terrain Three hills to climb, so considerable height to gain. All on access land, hence only animal paths in places. Farmland, so there will be sheep and some cows on all hills.
Refreshments *Ye Olde Royal Oak* in Wetton. Not always open midweek lunchtimes, but "toe wrestling" (believe it or not, now a World Championship event!) originated here.
When To Go/What's Here As all the hills and fields are extensively grazed, wild flowers are few; but Wetton village blossoms at daffodil-time. This is an exhilarating outing, especially in winter, when a dusting of snow on the hills transports the mind to higher ranges. As the height of all three hills only varies by 8 metres, geologists postulate this results from these coral-reef knolls being steadily eroded by ice (peneplanation). All three summits are crowned by Neolithic round barrows. Originally adorned with huge slabs of limestone, the sight of these white-topped hills must have been awesome. We pass over Pea Low, a chambered tomb almost unrecognisable now as such. Most of these monuments were ransacked by the fame-fed Thomas Bateman in the 1840/50s. Wetton church unusually has an external staircase to its belfry. Two early Carboniferous fossilised brachiopods were found in Narrowdale.

Wetlands beneath Wetton Hill (Aug 27)

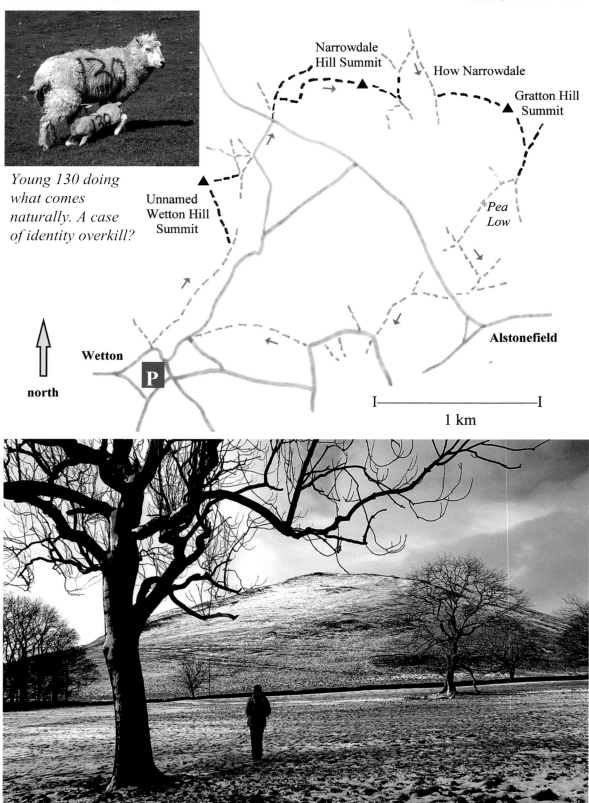

Young 130 doing what comes naturally. A case of identity overkill?

Narrowdale Hill Summit

How Narrowdale

Gratton Hill Summit

Unnamed Wetton Hill Summit

*Pea Low

Alstonefield

Wetton

P

north

I———————————I
1 km

Looking back to Wetton Hill from the path to Gateham Grange (Jan 1)

Route Turn left out of the car park and walk down the lane. Turn left at the T-junction, pass pub on left and keep ahead until the road turns 90° left. Here, take the track ahead and then turn right through the stile (footpath sign). The way ahead is clear to follow as the path first leads through fields to the left of a wall before continuing to the right of the wall. Four open fields are then crossed with stiles being in the middle of the walls ahead. After, bear left uphill to a stile and the access land on **Wetton Hill**. It is now best to start your ascent of the hill straight away, following the escarpment rightwards, uphill to the summit. Descend steeply from the summit, heading for a wall-stile just to the left of a narrow copse of trees. The path ahead leads to a lane. Turn left and follow it to a T-junction. Take the track ahead and, after about 150 m, turn right off the track onto access land and begin the ascent of **Narrowdale Hill**. At first, it is easiest to walk up just left of the wall which then dog-legs left and right whence, at last, you can make a push for the summit. From the top, you are heading down to a wall and a stile to the left of you. However, a direct descent is dangerous so angle right before veering left to the stile. The path ahead bears left and eventually spirals down to a short valley, **How Narrowdale**. Turn right, pass pump remains, go over stile and bear left, first following animal trails uphill and then going left to the summit of **Gratton Hill**. Descend the right flank of the hill, heading towards a building way below and to the right. Turn right at a track, cross cattle grid and walk past the building for about 100m to a stile on the right. Go over field to corner ahead. Through stile, follow wall on left to *Pea Low* (small hillock) and beyond over two fields to path X-roads. Turn left to track and right on it to side road, bearing right to road (left to **Alstonefield**). But over, just to left, go down track and then ahead on path to minor road. Turn right. After about ½ km, as road turns 90° left, follow the walled path until directed left off it over five more fields to **Wetton**.

Gratton Hill from Wetton Hill summit (Feb 27) **Inset.** *Cuckooflower near Pea Low*

Looking back to Narrowdale Hill from the lower flanks of Gratton Hill (Dec 7)

Two walkers on the summit of the unnamed Wetton Hill (July 22)

37 Deep Hayes Country Park, Caldon Canal and Cheddleton

The Roaches (left) and Hen Cloud from the top of Ladderidge Country Park (Nov 6)

This figure-of-eight walk links two scenic levels of the Caldon Canal, south of Leek, with two Country Parks and a Flint Mill. In summer, the stalwarts fire up the water-wheels!

Length 13 kms / 8.13 miles **Map** O/S Explorer OL 24, *White Peak Area*, West Sheet
Start/Finish Deep Hayes Country Park 4 kms SW Leek off the A53 at SJ 961 533. Buses from Leek/Stoke stop on A53 at entrance to Ladderidge CP at 973 551 where the walk can be picked up. Traveline 0970 6082 608 : Leek Tourist Information 01538 483725
Terrain There's a short but steep uphill plod out of Deep Hayes CP and a more gentle rise out of Ladderidge CP otherwise it's a level walk, mainly on paths and towpaths. It soon becomes muddy between Deep Hayes CP and Cheddleton, even after a little rain.
Refreshments *Old School Tearooms*; *Black Lion*; *Red Lion* at Cheddleton. Drinks at VC.
When To Go/What's There A walk for all seasons, but to see inside the Flint Mill and see the waterwheels in action go on summer weekends. There's more narrowboat activity on the canals, too. The mill is run by volunteers who will show you round or you can follow the "Flint Trail" from a leaflet. From the top of Ladderidge CP there's a view back to The Roaches and Hen Cloud. The Leek Branch of the Caldon Canal is the most picturesque. Leek Tunnel reopened in 1985. Here, a turning area has matured into a fine lake. On the far bank, heron and kingfisher hunt. Other birds seen include goosander, long-tailed tit, yellowhammer, goldfinch, green woodpecker, goldcrest, tufted duck, buzzard, sparrowhawk, kestrel, and red kites on a few occasions. Generally a heathland species, adders are in Deep Hayes CP along with grass snakes. There's a village pound and 12th century church passed at Cheddleton. Waterside plants include flowering rush, greater spearwort, reed canary-grass, water-dropwort and flag iris. Other flowers include teasel, greater butterfly-orchid, betony, foxglove, wood anemone and bluebell. Southern and brown hawker dragonflies and blue-tailed and common blue damselflies fly in July.

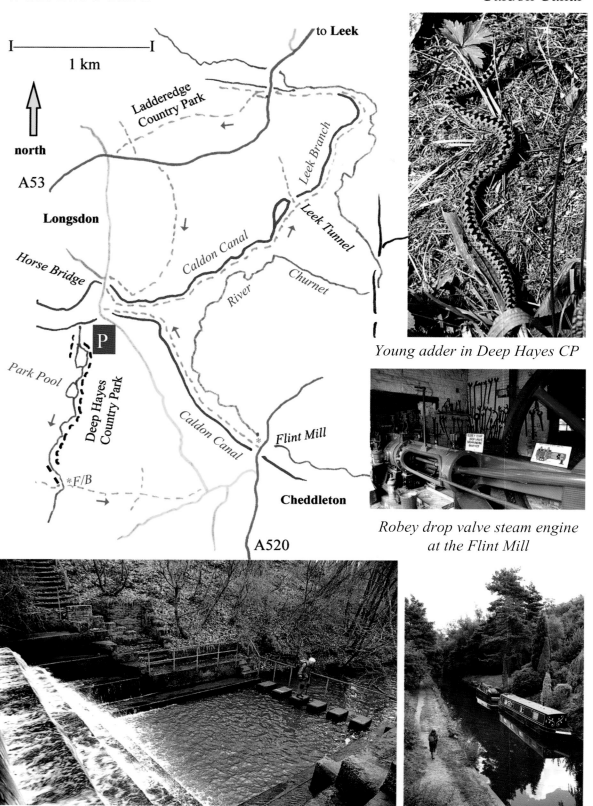

Young adder in Deep Hayes CP

Robey drop valve steam engine
at the Flint Mill

Above. *At the weir in Deep Hayes CP.* **Right.** *The canal from near Horse Bridge.*

Route Take the path left of the first lake and pass two other pools before entering woodland. The path ahead keeps left of the stream and crosses boarding and small bridges before reaching a footbridge proper over the stream. Over, bear left (red trail signs) to metal kissing gate and over boards. Bear right up steps and yet more to path T-junction. Turn left (footpath sign) go down steps and over footbridge. Keep ahead at junction (leave red signs) to gate/stile. Over, bear right then turn left up steep steps (seat at top!) to stile. Over, go to left corner of field, up short track and over four stiles left of farm to path X-roads over short plank and stiles with removable top bars. Now angle right of line of trees to wall stile and on to cross farm drive to road (Shaffalong Lane). Follow road ahead passing tea rooms, church and *Black Lion* to **A520** at **Cheddleton**. Turn left and soon left again to the ***Flint Mill*** and on to the ***Caldon Canal***. Follow towpath for about 1½ kms then rise up to road just before bridge No 39. Turn right up road to another canal which is accessed on the left. Turn right, go under bridge No 6 and follow the ***Leek Branch*** of the canal to ***Leek Tunnel***. Go up steps, cross track and follow towpath to its end. Don't enter ***Ladderidge CP*** but go over stile on left. Follow path by feeder stream to gate and on to fork. Go left to track. Turn right to the **A53**. Cross, take track left of milepost into car park and the left of two gates. Now keep ahead to a metal kissing-gate into wood. Immediately through, turn right uphill then left up to stile. Ahead, you are clearly directed to a drive. Turn left and left again down the **A53** for about 300m where extreme care has to be taken to cross the road to the signed footpath at Mollatts Wood Road. Ahead, the lane becomes a track then path down woodland. Take right fork at drive junctions and there are waymark signs on telegraph poles to lead you down to Sutherland Road. Turn left down the road to the Visitor Centre.

Some exhibits at the Flint Mill include Peak District millstones and grindstones.

A narrowboat negotiates a tight bend on the Caldon Canal, Leek Branch (July 27)

Discussing old times at the tiny Flint Mill cottages (July 27)

38 Milldale, Hall Dale, The Nabs and Baley Hill (Dove Dale North)

Looking into the chasm of Dove Dale with Alstonefield and Wetton Hill beyond (Jan 30)

In Walk The Peak we covered a high level route above south Dove Dale. Here, we have a similar escapade above the north of the dale. It's short, but involves considerable height to be gained, especially to The Nabs - an undulating ridge high above the valley bottom which leads to Baley Hill, and one of the finest all-round views in the White Peak.

Length 7 kms / 4.38 miles **Map** O/S Explorer OL 24, *White Peak Area*, West Sheet
Start/Finish Car parks at Milldale, 1 km SE of Alstonefield at SK 136 547. Go early.
Terrain Some paths are stony, others muddy when wet. In summer, there will be nettles on the way to The Nabs (poles?). Be warned! The ascent of the arête to The Nabs is very steep with sheer drops. The riverside path gives an easy finish if you balk at The Nabs.
Refreshments Polly's Cottage at Milldale in summer & winter weekends
When To Go/What's There Whatever the season, the scenery and views will impress. From the summit of The Nabs, walkers on the riverside path appear as dots. Up here is where the ravens and buzzards soar. You look across to Ravens Tor - aptly named for the birds nest here; look for the diamond-shaped tail to distinguish them in flight from crows/rooks. Dipper, grey wagtail and heron are on the river, but the iconic goosanders have been illegally erased by those with angling interests. Monkeyflower and great willowherb flower riverside. Meadows have yellow rattle, hawkweeds, marjoram, betony, harebell and fragrant orchids. The crags support wall rue, thyme, maidenhair spleenwort, rock-rose and biting stonecrop. Sadly, each year there are more nettles and fewer flowers. Great spotted woodpeckers drum and green ones cackle. Take binoculars to spot all the landmarks from Baley Hill. *Great willowherb (Aug 8)*

Monkeyflower by The Dove

On The Nabs ridge with Baley Hill beyond

Walkers on the riverside "Tourist Path", taken from Ilam Rock footbridge (Jan 30)

Route From the car parks walk east towards **Milldale**. 30m after *Bankside Cottage* on the right, turn right up the signed footpath. Ahead go through stile and ascend steep path which sustains its gradient until a gate in wall. Cross field to squeezer stile. To the left, **The Nabs** ridge is now in view. Ahead, walk through wall opening and on to stile/gate and fingerpost. Now follow long field left of wall to stile/gate and NT sign for **Grove Farm**. Walk ahead down track. After about 100m, turn left through gate/stile and angle right down field to gate/stile. Walk ahead left of wall to valley floor. Don't take gate/stile ahead but turn 90° left, following wall on right to step-stile. Over, go ahead to gate in wall and NT sign for start of **Hall Dale**. Follow grassy path to gate and on to stile. Path becomes stony (slippery when wet) and descends steeply to **River Dove**. Turn right (signed *Ilam Rock Bridge*); pass *Ilam* signpost to reach and cross **footbridge** at **Ilam Rock**. To see **Lion Rock** turn right for 200m or so, but our route turns left (signed *Milldale*). On, pass **Dove Holes** caves on right and, 70m on, it's decision-time: You can now see the summit crags of The Nabs above to the left so, if not for you, continue on riverside path to Milldale. If made of sterner stuff, turn right (signed *Alsop-en-le-Dale*). Path runs through nettles for 200m to gate/stile. A further 200m up path, at Access Land waymark post, turn left up very steep path on scree, later soil. Keep right of pinnacle ahead and then pass between stunted hawthorns on path, now less steep, up the arête. Near top path forks; go right. Follow path along the crest of **The Nabs**, over a stile and on to **Baley Hill** and the 360° viewpoint. On, descend to ladder stile and gate. Through, path forks; go left heading for gate in bottom corner of field. Don't go through but bear right through old wall then head ½ left down field to meet path coming in from right at a wall opening. Through, bear left down the wide, grassy path which leads scenically and later steeply down to **Viators Bridge** at Milldale.

In upper Hall Dale (Jan 30) **Inset.** *White form of fragrant orchid lower down (July 21)*

Top Left. *Approaching the summit ridge of The Nabs (Aug 8). The lower part of the arête is much steeper. You can avoid The Nabs by the level riverside path ...*

Top Right. *Meadowsweet and meadow cranes-bill on the "Tourist Path" close to Milldale (July 21).*

Left. *Passing Lion Rock (March 12). It looks "lion-ish" from both aspects.*

Above. *Stoat bringing down a rabbit in Hall Dale - a blurred lightning strike!*

39 Combes Valley NR, Brockholes, Basford Bridge and Fynneylane

Passing the summer-house at Brockholes (June 12)

This adventure, (and it is!) starts with a stroll through the RSPB reserve at Combes Valley; rises to Sharpcliffe Hall; passes quaint Brockholes before entering unforgiving Whitehough Wood. A more pleasant descent through another RSPB wood leads to an ancient cross and Basford Bridge. More uphill earns beautiful Fynneylane and Crowhalt.

Length 14 kms / 8.75 miles **Map** O/S Explorer OL 24, *White Peak Area*, West Sheet
Start/Finish The RSPB Nature Reserve car park at Combes Valley at SK 009 534, which is 5 kms south east of Leek and signposted off the A523 Ashbourne Road at SK 021 539
Terrain A mix of tracks, indistinct paths and woods - one of which you have to stoop to negotiate, and some roadwork. Animals are in fields. There is a very narrow footbridge!
Refreshments Complimentary tea/coffee at the RSPB Visitor Centre (and conveniences); tea rooms at Cheddleton Station (weekends), and the *Boat Inn* at Basford Bridge.
When To Go/What's There The RSPB spell their reserve Coombes; the O/S as above. Whatever, the reserve is justifiably proud in raising dozens of pied flycatchers in the nest boxes provided. The black and white birds are summer visitors. Other birds en route include buzzard, curlew, skylark, partridge, lapwing, green woodpecker, goldcrest, and a kingfisher flew under Basford Bridge. More often seen in garden centres, guelder rose is common in the reserve. Wet meadows near Crowhalt support wood horsetail, southern marsh and common spotted-orchid, marsh cinquefoil and ragged-robin, including an albino variety. We have counted eleven species of butterfly. You can treat the kids to a bird or insect badge at the Visitor Centre or perhaps a ride on the many themed specials run from Cheddleton Station on the Churnet Valley Railway (info 01538 360522). This interesting corner also has the Caldon Canal, ancient Basford Bridge and the *Boat Inn*.

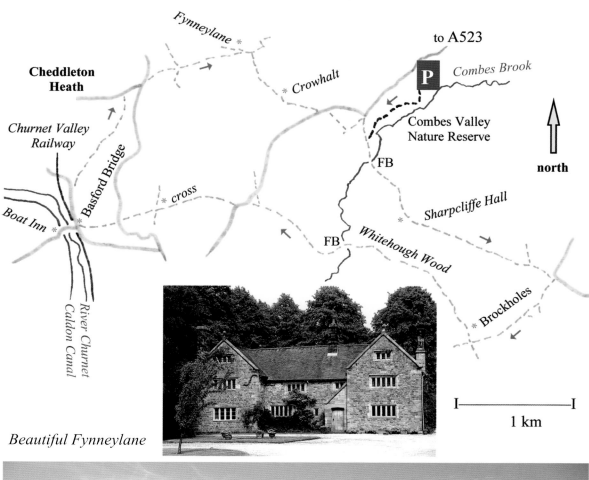

Beautiful Fynneylane

On the path through the RSPB Reserve at Combes Valley (June 12)

Route Go through gate in car park and head down track. Go through gate/stile then over footbridge across ***Combes Brook***. Bear left on track to stile left of building. At path junction, turn right, descend steps, cross footbridge and, at top of steps, turn left on public footpath up wood. A steep ascent leads to a field. Cross to gate near building. Turn left onto "drive". Pass ***Sharpcliffe Hall*** on right. Continue on lane for ½ km to X-roads. Turn right down track. After 1 km, keep left at junction. Then, before old barn, at junction of paths/tracks, turn right and go through stile. Cross field to stile. Cross drive of ***Brockholes*** to stile. Cross field to wall stile. Follow path right of wall down to stile. Cross field right of barn to makeshift bar stile. Over, take left path then keep left of wall; cross wet patch (waymark on tree on right) then bear left to pick up path left of trees to "stile" at entrance to ***Whitehough Wood***. Over, bear left and after 60m leave track to stile on right. Over, go ahead then soon left through rhododendrons. Follow path, indistinct at times, through low foliage. Out of it, keep ahead down overgrown track and go right, through gate. Cross field to gate and *RSPB* sign at wood. Follow "track" ahead then soon leave it and bear left down wood on a much more pleasant path than before, but to a very narrow-sided footbridge. Over, go up wood to stile then head up and across field to wall stile (waymark post). Cross field to stile in left corner. Over, bear right to stile and on to path between fence/hedge to metalled drive. Turn left then right over stile; then over another down to a road. Turn left. After 100m turn right beside *Lower House Farm* and follow track ahead to stile. Walk down field, right of wall, to ***cross*** and stile. Over, to another stile then on, right of hedge to road. Cross. Go over field to wall opening just left of building and stile ahead. Keep left of fence to track. Turn left to road. Now, left leads to Cheddleton Station, **Basford Bridge** and the ***Boat Inn***. However, our route turns right up the road (signed *Cheddleton* and *Leek*). After 300m, where a lane joins from the right, turn right over stile (signed *Cheddleton Heath*). Head up field to gap left of buildings; as work is in progress here, there may be an electric fence to cross. Look for blue "handle". Follow rough track ahead to concealed stile on right as track swings left. Over, head up field, about 50m left of trees ahead to stile in hawthorns at end of long, undulating field. Over, keep right of fence to drive and road. Turn right. At X-roads go ahead; pass *Yew Tree Farm* and on to ***Fynneylane*** (photo). Go through gate on right. After 30m, turn right to stile. Over, go down field to stile with post (and slab over stream). Over, angle up to top left of field and stile.

Crossing ancient Basford Bridge (Sept 27)

Head up to drive at ***Crowhalt***. Cross drive and on to meet it again. Bear left up drive and leave it at right bend and go over bridge/stile on left. Angle up to top left of field and stile. Over, head straight up field to stile right of buildings. Over is a road, so caution, here. Turn left and follow road to car park. Or, you could cross road, go up f/p and turn left into reserve again.

Top Left. *Deer at Upper Fernyhill.*
Top Right. *At the wayside cross.*
Left. *Ragged-robin grows in the nature reserve and also in damp fields near Crowhalt (all June 12).*

Fancy being a train driver? You can sometimes drive diesel engine number 37 075 for £10 at Cheddleton Station! **Inset.** *Guelder rose at Combes Valley Nature Reserve.*

Ilam Park, Rushley Bridge, Slade House and Musden Low

Having a peep at the trig pillar on Musden Low (Feb 7)

The alpine-styled hamlet of Ilam has attracted tourists for generations - for there is much to see and explore in the hamlet and adjacent park. Our walk visits all these "hotspots" and then rises to view fine panoramas which cradle the park in the valley below.

Length 10 kms / 6.3 miles **Map** O/S Explorer OL 24, *White Peak Area*, West Sheet
Start/Finish The National Trust car park in Ilam Park at SK 131 506 (Pay & Display)
Terrain Easy paths around Ilam Park together with paths up and down farmland, some of which may be indistinct or muddy. There may be livestock in some of the fields. Quite a lot of stiles of all sorts have to be negotiated. A few short stretches of minor roads.
Refreshments Tea rooms at the hall, not always open in winter. Conveniences may be.
When To Go/What's There Although quite short, there is quite a lot of (gentle) uphill to this walk for all seasons. Still, when you plummet downhill at the end of the trek you'll be glad this route was anticlockwise! And, to put it into perspective, downhill skiers fly down steeper ice than this at 90 mph! But we mortal walkers enjoy all that Ilam Park has to offer: There is a visitor centre; church with ancient cross; *St. Bertram's Well* where the resurgent River Manifold bubbles up and reappears after droughts; the stump of another ancient cross (info plaque) and the hamlet of unique architecture huddling beneath Bunster Hill. Ilam Cross is the Mary Watts-Russell Memorial erected by her heartbroken husband in 1841. It has 6 ornate statues. The original hall was partially demolished but saved and rebuilt to its current design. It is now a prestige Youth Hostel. An old lime kiln is passed. Maidenhair spleenwort is the new tenant. In winter, a huge flock of starlings swirl above the park before roosting on the outbuildings of Musden Grange. Holly blue, comma and brimstone butterflies flutter through the park in spring. Brown hares roam the high fields, and stoats the walls. Buzzards and kestrels roam the skies. Skylarks sing, too.

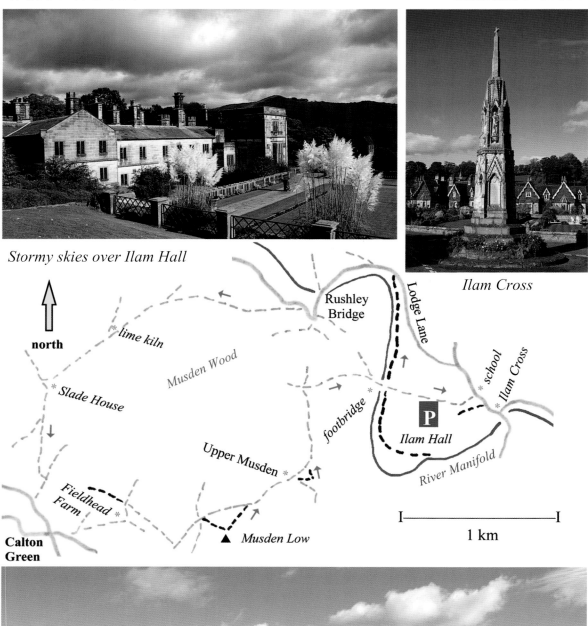

Stormy skies over Ilam Hall

Ilam Cross

On the way back through Ilam Park, heading to Thorpe Cloud, right (Oct 18)

Route Walk into the grounds of **Ilam Hall** from the car park and take path or steps down to the **River Manifold**. Turn right and follow riverside path past railed *St. Bertram's Well* and the stump of the cross. Ignore **footbridge** on the left, but go through gate and follow river until path reaches **Lodge Lane**. Turn left. Road bears left, crosses **Rushley Bridge** and does a hairpin right. 100m after, turn left off road and angle right of trees up to gate in wall and then wall-steps (post) in right corner of next field. Bear right and keep left of wall for two fields then angle left to gate in wall. Through, keep just right of wall in what becomes a very long field (800m), passing the ***lime kiln*** in a hollow on the right, before reaching stile and gate. On, keep right of building and turn left down track to gate right of ***Slade House***. Pass wall corner on left and keep right of wall to gate. Through, path forks. Take left fork and follow path just right of hedge/wall down the long field (400m), angling left at the bottom to a gate. Through, keep ahead to road at **Calton Green**. Turn left and left again at X-roads (seat), signed to *Ashbourne*. After 100m turn left off road and angle left over field to twin stiles and on to farm drive. Turn left, go through two gates to left corner of field (wall stile, yellow post). Ahead to wall stile (yellow on pole) and on to gate and farm track at ***Fieldhead Farm***. Turn left down track and after about 150m, at left bend, leave track over the rightmost of two wooden stiles, about 10m apart. Go up field right of wall. Just before end of field, and after an opening, go left over stile in wall. Go ahead then angle a little right, up to stile. Over, to have a peep at the **trig pillar**, turn right up to top of field, where the pillar is over a wall. Now turn left to bottom right of field. Through the stile keep left of wall and go right through opening (fingerpost). Bear left, go over two ladder stiles right of ruins at **Upper Musden**. On, as wall turns 90° left, follow wall to stile on left. From here, head down right of wall to gate/ladder stile. Ahead, after about 300m, turn right, very steeply downhill to wall stile and on through another to footbridge. Over, cross path and walk ahead up parkland. Head towards Thorpe Cloud to pick up a track to a gate. Turn right and go through the gate left of park entrance back into the park.

Over the ladder stiles at the ruins of Upper Musden (Feb 7)

Looking back to Bunster Hill (left) and pyramidal Thorpe Cloud (Feb 7)

The walk arrives at Ilam School, with its decidedly alpine appearance (Oct 18)

Walks On White Peak Map ——————— East Sheet

(Explorer Outdoor Leisure Series No 24)

There are a series of fine wildlife pools near to the oldest surviving industrial chimney in Britain (c 1770) and to walk 46 (Aug 24). They are beside a footpath at SK 335 669.

41 Foxlane Plantation, Barbrook Reservoir and Ramsley Moor

Looking over to Big Moor from the path across Ramsley Moor (Oct 17)

An easy ramble through the Eastern Moors with much wildlife and ancient sites to see. The remaining water in the drained reservoirs of Barbrook and Ramsley have matured into fine wildlife pools. Along with Leash Fen and Big Moor, the moors on our walk were in great jeopardy until the owners accepted a joint bid by the RSPB and National Trust.

Length 10 kms / 6.25 miles **Map** O/S Explorer OL 24, *White Peak Area*, East Sheet
Start/Finish Shillito Wood car park off the A621, 5 kms NE of Baslow at SK 295 749
Terrain Easy to follow tracks and paths. Very little uphill.
Refreshments None on route. Café and pubs in Baslow. *Peacock Inn* at Owler Bar.
When To Go/What's There A walk for all seasons; beautiful when the heather is out and equally so in autumn when the moor-grasses turn golden. Then, Big Moor resembles an African plain. Two stone circles are met. The most complete circle, with 22 stones of fairly equal size lies at SK 28336 77289 (GPS acc to 3m). Two ancient wayside crosses are passed. Two guide stoops are also passed: One on the way to Barbrook Reservoir is unusual in that the inscriptions are Shefield "*Way*" etc instead of the usual "*...Roade*" as per other guide stoops in The Peak. The red deer herd, escapees from Chatsworth, now number in excess of 30. Males can be heard calling in October before the rut. These moors are an adder stronghold in The Peak. Corrugated iron sheets have been placed to entice the reptiles to the warmth beneath. Lizards, adder prey, are common in summer. In June and July, the golden-ringed dragonfly hawks up and down Bar Brook. A northern species of water beetle, *Agabus arcticus*, is also found at Bar Brook. It, too, has a golden ring. Pools support emerald and large-red damselfly, emperor, common hawker, four-spot chaser and black darter dragonfly. Curlew, snipe, skylark, stonechat, great spotted woodpecker, kestrel and sparrowhawk are observed. Bog flushes have *Sphagnum* moss, bog pondweeds and water-crowfoot. Sheep's sorrel and bluebells flower in spring.

Above. *Passing Barbrook Little Reservoir (Oct 5)*

Middle. *Sheep and red deer tracks leading to the pools in the drained Barbrook Reservoir. In parts, the sandy bottom of the reservoir has an almost desert-like appearance, but this will soon change when the vegetation colonizes (Oct 5, 2008)* **Bottom left.** *The invasive Spanish bluebell adds a splash of colour to Foxlane Plantation in spring (May 22)* **Bottom Right.** *The damaged ancient wayside cross at the start of the walk (May 22)*

Jittery red deer hinds opposite the first guide post (May 22).

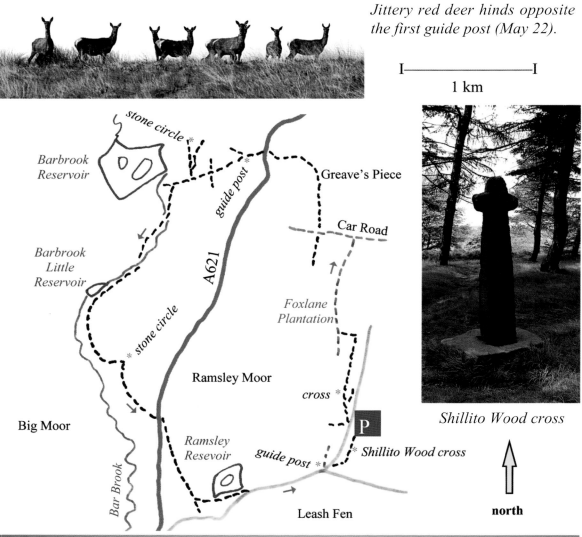

I———————————I
1 km

Shillito Wood cross

↑
north

The wildlife pool that now remains in Ramsley Reservoir (Oct 17)

Route Walk out of the car park, cross the road and turn right. After about 20 metres there is a gate on the left. Turn right immediately through the gate on the path parallel to the road. It soon forks so keep left to the *cross*, visible ahead. Take the left path from the cross and follow it to a fence and locked gate. Turn left and follow the steep path down to the main path through **Foxlane Plantation**. Turn right and follow the path to a stony track, which is **Car Road**. Turn left up the track. After about 200 metres go over the stile on the right. The way ahead meanders pleasantly through **Greave's Piece** to the **A621**. Cross the road and walk up the metalled track, passing a **guide post** on the left. When nearly at a building, there is a gate on the right. Go through the gate to view the wildlife pools in **Barbrook Reservoir**. Return and go through gate. From here, a track leads 30° northish. Go up the track. After about 40 metres it forks. Take the narrower left fork. After about another 250 metres, the largest (in area) **stone circle** is found on the right, about 20 metres from the path. Return to the gate. Over the track a path runs south to **Barbrook Little Reservoir**. Further on, at a conspicuous bend, the smaller **stone circle** can be seen a few metres up to the left. There is a cairn above the circle. The path ahead leads to a stile and the A621 again. Cross and go over the stile on to a path which leads over **Ramsley Moor** to a fence at **Ramsley Reservoir**. Walk beside the fence, just under a grassy headwall to its eastern end, where a stile gives access for a peep at the pool. From the stile a path leads to a wall stile, gate and minor road. Turn left up the road to a junction after 400 metres. Here, on the left, over the wall (gate for access) is another **guide post** in a wet patch. Take the left road fork. After a few metres take the path on the right through Shillito Wood. Keep right at junctions and then left to reach the *cross* in the trees and on to the car park.

The largest stone at the smaller circle (Oct 17). Pagan offerings are often left here.

Holmesfield, Barlow Common, Rumbling Street and Millthorpe

A herd of inquisitive youngsters in a field at Peakley. So, if you don't like cows ...

This walk full of variety passes Cartledge Hall then descends through unimproved old fields to woodland and between two fine lakes to Barlow Common. Here, "improved" fields lead to the hamlet of Johnnygate; a ford at Millthorpe, and a climb to Holmesfield.

Length 11 kms / 6.88 miles **Map** O/S Explorer OL 24, *White Peak Area*, East Sheet
Start/Finish Car park behind St Swithin's church at Holmesfield, off the B6054 at SK 320 777. The car park is reserved for the congregation on Sundays between 9am to noon, otherwise you are welcome. Buses from Chesterfield stop on Mill Lane at the *Travellers Rest* at the start of the walk. Traveline 0870 6082 608. Train info 08457 484950.
Terrain Mainly farmland paths, some muddy. Animals in fields. A few gentle climbs.
Refreshments Lots!: *George & Dragon*; *The Angel* and Thai restaurant at Holmesfield. The *Tickled Trout*; *Fox & Hounds* at Barlow Common. *Royal Oak* at Millthorpe.
When To Go/What's There Information boards at Holmesfield and Millthorpe relate the history of the area. Millthorpe has a ford garlanded with snowdrops in spring. The hamlet dress their well in July near to a plaque commemorating a nearby Meteor crash in 1955. Grass snakes and common carp swim the lakes. Swan, little grebe, coot, tufted duck and moorhen paddle them. Eight species of dragonfly breed including emperor, southern and brown hawker, common darter and four-spot chaser. The woods have ramsons, bluebells, wood anemones, celandines, dog's mercury, wood spurge, wild honeysuckle, squirrels, and green and great spotted woodpeckers. On the way back to Holmesfield you pass through a fine wild flower field with betony, common spotted-orchid, yellow rattle, oxeye daisy, rock-rose, knapweed and meadow vetchling. These attract small skipper, meadow brown, peacock, wall, gatekeeper, orange-tip and small copper butterflies.

The brown hawker breeds at the lakes. From a painting of the male by the author (life x 1¼)

Left. *Meadow brown butterfly on betony at Millthorpe.* **Above.** *Common carp are visible in the lakes.*
Below. *Approaching Holmesfield.*

In the fields from Johnnygate down to Millthorpe (July 13)

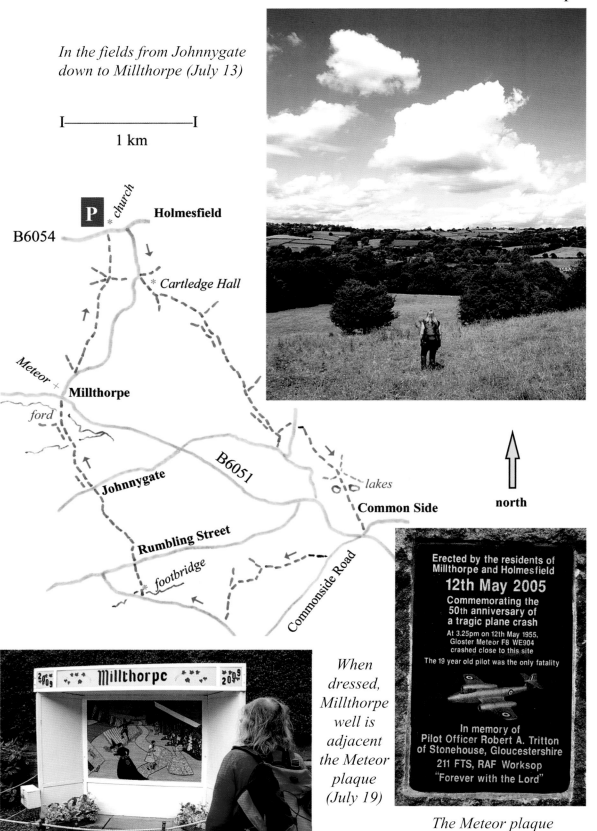

I————————I
1 km

B6054

P *church*

Holmesfield

Cartledge Hall

Meteor +

Millthorpe

ford

B6051

Johnnygate

Rumbling Street

footbridge

Common Side

lakes

Commonside Road

north

When dressed, Millthorpe well is adjacent the Meteor plaque (July 19)

Erected by the residents of
Millthorpe and Holmesfield
12th May 2005
Commemorating the
50th anniversary of
a tragic plane crash
At 3.25pm on 12th May 1955,
Gloster Meteor F8 WE904
crashed close to this site
The 19 year old pilot was the only fatality

In memory of
Pilot Officer Robert A. Tritton
of Stonehouse, Gloucestershire
211 FTS, RAF Worksop
"Forever with the Lord"

The Meteor plaque

Route Turn left out of car park to the **B6054**. Turn left and cross the road before the mini-roundabout at the Travellers Rest. Go down Cartledge Lane and pass *Cartledge Hall* on left and continue ahead down the bridleway, soon to leave it at a wall stile on the left. Over, go down long field right of fence/wall and through a chain-stile. Now angle 45° right to another such stile. Cross track and head through a 3rd chain-stile and follow path left of bridleway to wall-stile and on down long field to gate/stile to rejoin bridleway. After 80m, turn left down drive and up steps left of dwelling to stiles and steps and on to a lane. Turn right, cross lane (seat) and go up track on left. After 80m turn right into wood and follow path down to a much waymarked post on left. Turn right through stile and take path between two lakes; go over footbridge to track. Head up track. After 30m, go over stile on left and head up fields left of hedge to steps and lane. Turn right. Cross **B6051** and head up **Commonside Road**. Just past *Hare & Hounds* turn right down Mods Lane and go over stile ahead into field. Cross another field and ahead go through opening in hedge. Turn immediately left to another opening. Turn right to stile. Over, path later bears left to gate/ stile. Ahead, ignore wall opening on right but head up middle of field to gate/stile and another to lane. Turn right. After 600m, close to bottom of hill, turn right (wall stile) and head over **footbridge**, then left of fabulous old oak; up two fields left of hedge to **Rumbling Street**. Turn right then left through farm and down track, left of hedge and on into wood. Path bears right to stile then left of hedge to lane. Turn right then left. After a few metres, don't take signed bridleway left, but right of this, go through gate (huge eucalyptus on left) and go down long field, right of hedge, to stile and footbridge over stream. Onwards keep right of hedge to stile/gate. Turn right down lane, cross **ford** at **Millthorpe** and go up to and cross the B6051. Go up Millthorpe Lane. After 200m go left to stile right of gate (not left to f/b). Follow path up fields just right of trees and then left to hidden f/b and stiles, then path up long meadow to stile at the top. Go up field left of woodland to stile just on from 5-way finger post and continue ahead to track and gates/stiles to **Holmesfield**.

At Johnnygate (July 13)

43 Longstone Moor, White Rake, Rough Side and Longstone Edge

Looking over to Wardlow Hay Cop (see p. 230) from White Rake's molehills (Feb 2)

Take a walk over the greatest expanse of limestone heath in The Peak before it's too late! Under threat from mining interests (in reality, quarrying limestone) until 2042 this precious habitat fortunately has friends, especially when the National Park Authority seems powerless. The walk ends with aerial views of Coombes Dale and Great Longstone.

Length 11 kms / 6.88 miles **Map** O/S Explorer OL 24, *White Peak Area*, East Sheet
Start/Finish A number of lay-bys beside the minor road that runs parallel to Longstone Edge at SK 201 730. Best approached from Great Longstone, 1½ kms to the south.
Terrain Mainly paths and tracks over moor and farmland; slippery/muddy after rain.
Refreshments None on route. *Crispin* and *White Lion* inns at Gt Longstone may be open
When To Go/What's There To drive down the minor road with the car park lay-bys from east to west is like landing in a plane. One lady in 2008 must have thought so as her car left this road, and it was two days before she was seen and rescued (unhurt) from her vehicle stuck in trees far below! On the pretext of mining fluorspar and barytes, millions of tons of limestone have been removed, creating an artificial canyon at High Rake. Great crested newts, a protected species, breed in pools on the moor and have been cited in attempts to halt the march of the quarry. In contrast, Cavendish Mill has a bird hide at a mature settling lagoon where members of the Bakewell & District Bird Study Group can observe many visiting waders. Orchids grow unmolested at the mill. However, the orchid underworld is illegally uprooting dark-red helleborines from a site on this walk. The moor supports lizard, mountain pansy, skylark, grouse, snipe and wheatear. Pools have five species of dragonfly and over forty species of water beetle. Elsewhere on the walk, spring sandwort, thyme, maidenhair spleenwort, trefoils, limestone fern, kidney vetch, cowslip, crosswort, early-purple orchid, southern marsh-orchid, common spotted-orchid, fly orchid, harebell and rock-rose flower. Curlew, redshank and common sandpiper visit the wetlands. For news of the plight of the moor visit www.longstone-edge.org.uk

Longstone Moor (Aug 14), wild and lofty as it should be, and ...

... what will happen to it if the opencast mining (quarrying, really) interests are given the green light to extend High Rake (above). The huge, yellow dumper sets the scale.

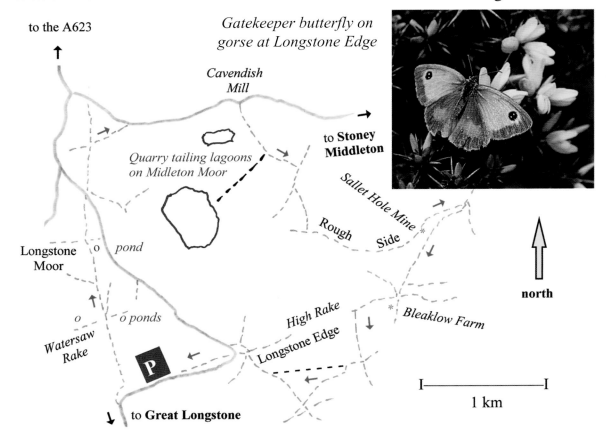

to the A623

Gatekeeper butterfly on gorse at Longstone Edge

Cavendish Mill

to **Stoney Middleton**

Quarry tailing lagoons on Midleton Moor

Sallet Hole Mine

Rough   Side

Longstone Moor

o *pond*

north

o   o *ponds*

High Rake

Bleaklow Farm

Watersaw Rake

Longstone Edge

P

1 km

to **Great Longstone**

Looking down on walkers in Coombes Dale **Inset.** *Fly orchids in the dale (both June 18)*

Route From the lay-by walk west down the road. Cross cattle-grid. Ignore first gate on right and just after left bend turn right through gate. Follow path steeply uphill through wood to stile. Follow path ahead over **Longstone Moor**. Cross "track" and keep ahead on path to wall stile. Onwards to another. Over, angle a little right to another wall stile. Cross field ahead to stile and road. Cross. Go through gate ahead and field to another gate. Cross track. Go over stile ahead and pass an isolated stile to another stile at a fence on **White Rake**. Over, proceed to wall stile with solitary tree just left. Over, don't take path ahead, but turn half right and head up large field (bearing 70°) between small rock outcrops and on to ladder stile. Over, angle left to stile (fossils) and road. Turn right to **Cavendish Mill**. Turn right at the footpath sign and cross footbridge. Head up track. As main track swings right, turn left and enter field. Keep just right of wall/fence to stile or gate and track. Turn right. After about 150m turn left at

fingerpost and gate. Head down field just right of wall. Near the valley bottom, angle right to stile at fence. Over, turn left down track. Follow track for nearly 1½ kms beneath **Rough Side**, passing *Sallet Hole Mine* entrance on right and on to large boulders either side of track. Immediately turn right over plank to stile. (Don't go a little further down track to fingerpost - wrong path). As path ahead appears to fork keep right and follow path as it rises high above the dale to a gate and on to a stile. Over, bear right to stile left of barn; then two more to main track at **High Rake**. Turn right. After about 300m turn left down the stony, walled track. Pass a gate on the right to a stile on the right. Over, angle right, away from wall on left up to track. Follow track ahead along **Longstone Edge** and beneath a beech wood. Track then bears right, uphill, to twin stiles. Go over left one. Pass stile on right and go to road. Turn left down road to lay-bys.

Southern marsh-orchids at Cavendish Mill (June 18)

44 Linacre Reservoirs, Birley Brook, Frithhall Wood and Old Brampton

On the path beside the south bank of the upper reservoir (June 9)

Linacre Reservoirs were constructed between 1855 and 1904 to supply water for the Chesterfield area. These days, the Linacre Valley Project is a loose partnership between Severn Trent, Derbyshire County Council Countryside Service, and the local community to provide a wildlife and heritage experience. We also visit the surrounding countryside.

Length 10 kms / 6.25 miles **Map** O/S Explorer OL 24, *White Peak Area*, East Sheet
Start/Finish The Linacre Reservoir complex has three car parks. The walk starts from the bottom CP where there is a *Welcome* board and tree sculpture. The reservoirs are accessed via a lane off the B6050, 1 km west of Cutthorpe at SK 333 733. The route passes through Old Brampton where there is a bus stop at the church and *George and Dragon*. Buses between Bakewell and Chesterfield (170) stop here, so you could start the walk from here. Traveline (the number constantly changes) to date is 0870 609 2608.
Terrain Easy to follow paths around the reservoirs. Some paths through the surrounding farmland may be muddy after rain. A little roadwork on pavements. Very little uphill.
Refreshments *Royal Oak* and *George & Dragon* on route. 100m detour to *Fox & Goose*.
When To Go/What's There In spring the woods reveal bluebells, ramsons, stitchwort and yellow archangel. The bat and bird boxes are well used. Amphibious bistort is colonizing the reservoirs and attracts the red-eyed damselfly. When the grassy headwalls are mown, woodpeckers may be seen feeding on the disturbed insects. There's the odd cormorant, heron and mandarin duck. May is a good time to see coot, grebe, tufted duck and mallard chicks. In winter, waterfowl migrants appear as do a few crossbills and goldcrests in the pines. Meadows have yellow rattle, ox-eye daisy and common spotted-orchid. The farmland sports gorse, foxglove, lapwing, skylark, rabbit, buttercup and brown hare. The scrub has wild honeysuckle, bittersweet, tufted vetch, rowans, dog rose and common gromwell. On the walk we have observed seven species of butterfly.

Top Left. *Part of Jason Thomson's millennium wood sculpture in the lower car park.*

Above. *Ever seen a coot's feet? We hadn't until this guy attacked us on the boarding of the upper reservoir in mid May! The pair had young close-by and were very aggressive.*

Below. *The stepping stones across Birley Brook (July 10).* **Inset.** *5-spot burnet moth on common spotted-orchid in the damp flushes of the meadow that follows (July 10).*

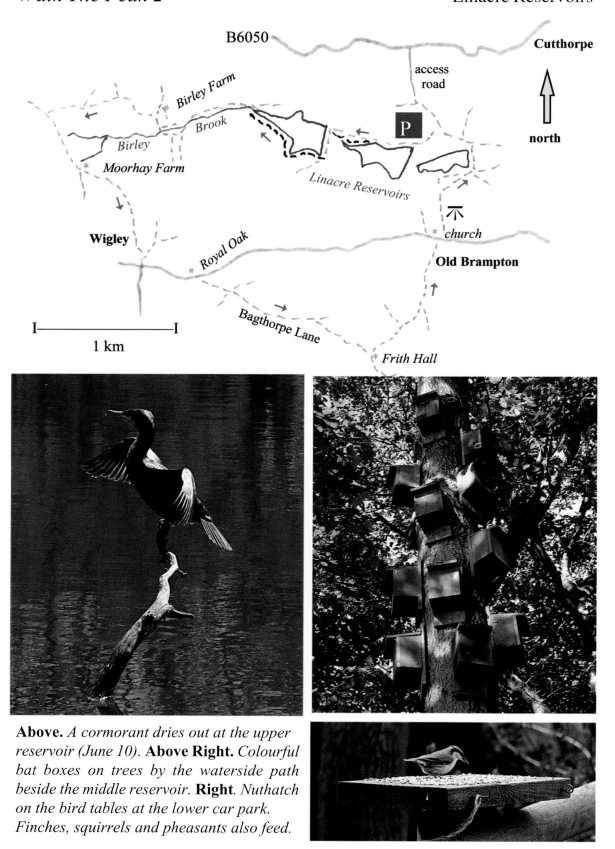

Above. *A cormorant dries out at the upper reservoir (June 10).* **Above Right.** *Colourful bat boxes on trees by the waterside path beside the middle reservoir.* **Right.** *Nuthatch on the bird tables at the lower car park. Finches, squirrels and pheasants also feed.*

Route Go down the path just left of the *Welcome* sign and turn right at the bottom. This leads to the headwall of the middle reservoir. Take the path to the right of the reservoir. After some picnic tables there is a gate on the left. You now have a choice of either going through the gate and following the waterside path through woodland (bat boxes) or staying on the main path, passing more wood sculptures. Both routes lead to the upper reservoir. Turn left across this headwall and then right, to follow the waterside path which eventually crosses **Birley Brook** by a footbridge. Turn left after the bridge and follow the path through woodland to a wall and gate. Onwards the path leads to stepping stones over the brook and through meadows to a stile/stone bridge over the brook. Turn right as soon as you cross the water and the path swings right and leads up to **Birley Farm**. Walk up the drive and after about 70m go through the gate on the left. Follow path across field to gate. Here, turn left through stile, pass overgrown quarries on left then turn left on a drive. Pass Freebirch House on right and head on to a track junction (signpost). Turn sharp left on grassy track which runs beside arable fields to an opening in the left corner. The way now leads down into woodland and on to a track at **Moorhay Farm**. Turn left (signpost) and walk on the track until a minor road is met at **Wigley**. Turn right to meet another road. Cross carefully and walk down the pavement for about 300m until the ***Royal Oak*** appears over the road. Turn right down **Bagthorpe Lane** opposite the pub, pass The Birches on the left. Just before **Frith Hall**, with its ancient crook barn, is a pond on the right and, opposite, a stile. Walk down the right side of the field. At the bottom the path bears left and up to a stile to enter Frithhall Wood. The path leads to two footbridges. Go over the right one, bear right and exit the wood. Turn left, follow path right of hedge/wall, go through a wall and turn left. There now follows two fields with stiles in their left corner. After them, angle right across field to wall stile left of buildings. Over, follow paths to road at **Old Brampton**. Cross road, turn right to **church**. Enter churchyard via the lychgate and walk right of church to stile and, ahead, another (benchmark). Walk down field to stile. Over, bear right on path through middle of field (photo below) to a stile. Over, go ahead and down; cross headwall of lower reservoir and walk up steps to lane (conveniences). Bear left up to the car park.

The path back through barley fields to Lower Linacre Reservoir (June 10)

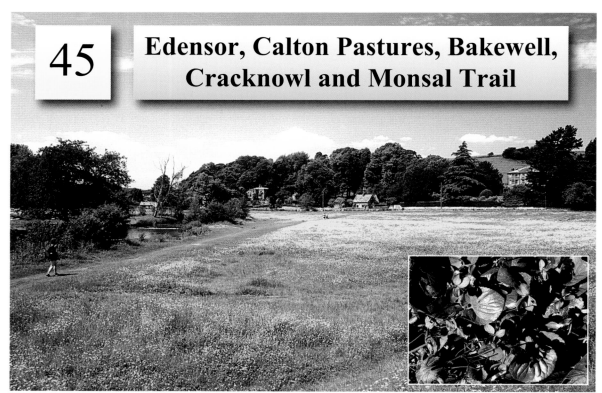

Buttercup-time beside the River Wye on the way to Holme Hall and Cracknowl (May 18).
Inset. *Sweet violets (var. praecox) beside the track to Edensor (March 20).*

This circuit of the north and east flanks of Bakewell, with fine views over the town and its environs, begins by climbing ancient Ball Cross Wood before descending to picturesque Edensor. The way then rises to Calton Pastures before descending more woods to a riverside walk leading to Holme Hall, Cracknowl, and a stroll back on The Monsal Trail.

Length 13 kms / 8.13 miles **Map** O/S Explorer OL 24, *White Peak Area*, East Sheet
Start/Finish Bakewell Station car park (P&D) at the top of Station Road at SK 222 689. Bakewell is well served by buses from Derby, Buxton, Sheffield and Chesterfield.
Terrain Easy to follow paths and tracks over farmland; through woods and the flat track of a short section of the *Monsal Trail*. A little roadwork. The A619 is crossed. A short but steep descent of woodland on a rocky/slippery path has to be taken with care.
Refreshments Tea rooms, Edensor; Hassop Station; Bakewell itself for puddings etc
When To Go/What's There A walk for all seasons. Edensor village is unique in that all the dwellings have a different design. The old school plaque lies on the village green. A 300 year-old guide stoop is passed. Two golf warning bells can be zealously rung! The wooden *Russian Cottage* was a gift to the 6th Duke of Devonshire from Tsar Nicholas I. As you rise over Cracknowl, a footpath leads left to *Cracknowl House*. Known locally as *"Artists Cottage"* this isolated dwelling was home to artist Bert Broomhead for many decades. Artist currently in residence is Russell Sim. Bakewell carnival is the best in The Peak; first Sat in July. A fine packhorse bridge is seen opposite Holme Hall. In the hedge here, a kingfisher "slept" for many years. You pass herds of red and fallow deer on the way from Edensor to Calton Pond. Here, snipe feed. Frogs, newts, dragonflies and water forget-me-not also flourish. Woodcock, skylark, woodpeckers, buzzard and partridge breed locally. Owls hoot in Manners Wood. Black-headed gulls sit on Bakewell Bridge!

Top. *Alpacas on the path down to Bakewell (March 20).*

Above. *Patriotic rafters tackle a weir on the River Wye at Bakewell. The raft race is on the Thursday eve preceding the carnival (first Sat in July).*

Left. *Edensor church (Sept 9)*

Longstone Edge (Walk 43) from Cracknowl (Oct 7)

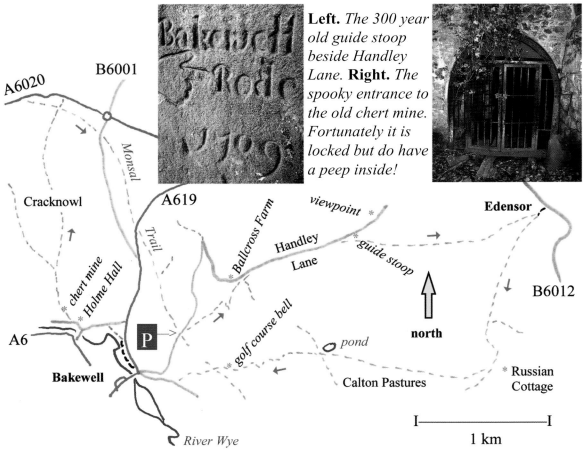

Left. *The 300 year old guide stoop beside Handley Lane.* **Right.** *The spooky entrance to the old chert mine. Fortunately it is locked but do have a peep inside!*

High and exposed Calton Pond **Inset.** *Bolbitius fungi in the nearby fields (both 15 Oct)*

Route Turn left out of the CP and left again up the lane. After about 100 metres take the signed path on the right. The bridleway crosses a couple of tracks and a golf bell (for horse-riders) on route to Ball Cross Wood. Near top of wood the eroded path crosses track and emerges at **Handley Lane** right of *Ballcross Farm*. Head up lane. After 800m, go down track on right. At this junction is the *guide stoop*, the dated face being lane-side (fine *viewpoint* 200m down the lane). Follow track down. More than a km later it reaches **Edensor**. Before the church and Stephens Cottage take the signed path on the right; up steps to gate and into field. Head half-right to waymark post and continue in this same southerly direction to just right of a fenced wood where path becomes clearer up to waymark post and on to wall steps and opening gate (seats, views). Follow track ahead between woodland to gate/stile. Over, walk ahead on track and after 80m turn right off track (signpost, *Russian Cottage* behind you). Head between plantations to and through gate/stile. Keep ahead and after about 300m drop down to slabs and stone trough. Now keep ahead just right of fence and up to gate just before the *pond* on **Calton Pastures**. Walk beside pond and go through gate. Take left path (signed *Bakewell*) on fence. Head down field; underneath power lines to gate in wall. Follow path down. It crosses track at square stone water relic and becomes stony as it runs downhill. Keep ahead at branch-path on left (*Haddon Estates Walk*, sign). Out of wood, pass *golf course bell*. Bear left to cross *Monsal Trail* via bridge and into field (alpacas, right). Walk down to road. Turn right. Cross to left footpath and to fountain. Carefully cross **A619** to gate and Scot's Garden, before **Bakewell** Bridge, left. Follow riverside path through twin gates to lane. Turn left then right up track opposite the packhorse bridge. Pass *Holme Hall* and then the *chert mine* (under girders) to gate. Field leads to stone stile and walled track which is followed over **Cracknowl** and down to the *Monsal Trail*. Turn right and stroll the 2 kms back to the car park at Bakewell Station.

A stormy day at Edensor (Jan 31) **Inset.** *Red deer on the way up to New Piece Wood*

46

Beeley Moor, Longside Moor, Harewood Moor and Fallinge Edge

The view from Fallinge Edge is well worth the short detour over access land (Oct 4)

This fairly long but not too strenuous outing starts with a visit to a stone circle; rises to another ancient site before lofty, easy walking over Beeley Moor leads to a descent of Longside Moor to Harewood Grange and a traverse of Harewood Moor itself. This is prime guide stoop country and some old boundary posts may also kindle an interest.

Length 13 kms / 8.13 miles **Map** O/S Explorer OL 24 *White Peak Area*, East Sheet
Start/Finish Roadside/trackside parking at a 90° bend on Beeley Lane at SK 287 680, most busy on Sundays. Space must be left for estate vehicles to pass through the track. There is a limited bus service to Beeley, which would add a further 5 kms to the walk.
Terrain Largely easy to follow (and find) paths over the moors with a little roadwork.
Refreshments None on route but the *Devonshire Arms* at Beeley is not too far away.
When To Go/What's There The boggy flushes on Beeley Moor are one of the few places in The Peak where the insectivorous round-leaved sundew is to be found - but the plants here are much smaller than in the south of the country and hence more difficult to find. Merlin and hobby are two raptors that hunt on the moor, the latter being most noticeable when there is an explosion in the population of oak eggar moths. Buzzards and goshawks breed locally but all four are again being shot, probably because black grouse have been seen since 2008. Other birds include kestrel, lapwing, curlew, skylark, snipe, an occasional cuckoo in summer and crossbill and goldcrest in the pines in winter. Brown hares roam the agricultural land and stoats the walls. We have seen lizards on Harewood Moor, but as yet no adders. Common hawker dragonflies breed in watery ditches. There is a stone circle of sorts passed at SK 28053 68509 (GPS ref) and the unusual tumulus of *Hob Hurst's House* has an information board. There are two fine guide stoops passed en route, with a third being just a 1½ km road detour (see map and photo). Plants include ling and bell heather, cross-leaved heath, bilberry, foxglove and hare's-tail cottongrass.

Down the lane at the start of the walk, with Beeley Moor above (Feb 10)

Left. *The guide stoop beneath the trig pillar on Beeley Moor. The spelling of the destinations on such posts was determined by the width of the stone and, to a certain extent, the literacy of the stonemason; hence "Shefeld" for Sheffield. But at least the travellers of old had a direction to follow. There are three other inscriptions on the post, to "Backwell", "Worksworth" and "Chestierfeld".* **Above.** *The boundary stone at the end of Harewood Moor has weathered crosses in circles depicting the Earth symbol, but is not at any parish boundary.*

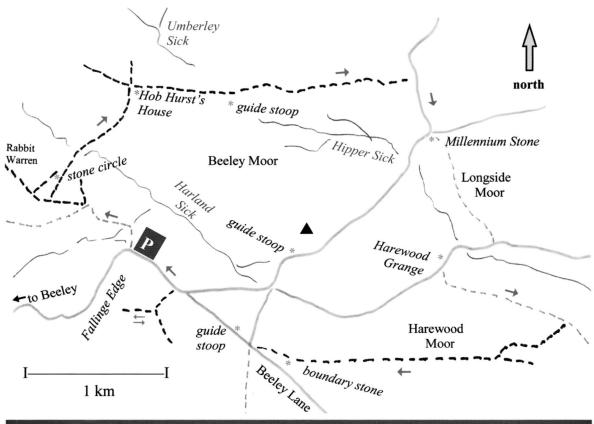

Looking back to Harewood Moor (Feb 10)

Route Walk north down the lane. 400m later, at the second 90° left bend, go over the high wall step-stile ahead. Walk up track. The incline eases and the track then runs straight. After 300m, just before track bends right, turn right on faint 4x4 track over moor. After 200m the *stone circle* is on the left. Later, paths join but keep ahead, cross stream and go over wall step-stile, right of gate. Follow path beside wood to top. Take right path; soon *Hob Hurst's House* tumulus is on the right a little off main path. Onwards, there's a *guide stoop* on the right (photo below). Continue ahead on path to stile and road. Turn right. Follow road for ½ km to T-junction. Cross; go through gate by *Millennnium Stone* and follow bridleway ahead across the long field, using the waymarked posts as guide. At end of field path descends **Longside Moor** to gate and road. Turn right. After 100m, there's another 2000AD boundary stone on the left. 70m after *Harewood Grange* on the right, turn left down the bridleway. Opposite the dwelling, turn left through twin gates and follow the path up the moor for a km to meet a gate in wall corner. Don't go through but back-track about 20m to pick up a 4x4 track that runs SW up the heather moor. At the top of the moor track swings right and

descends to meet another vestigial track. Bear right and follow the track for 2 kms over **Harewood Moor** (one gate or stile to negotiate) to stile and road junction. Take second right (NW). After 200m, there's a *guide stoop* on the right. Keep ahead at a junction then, 50m on, if you want the view from **Fallinge Edge**, go over wall step-stile on the left; follow track until it turns 90° left but you go 90° right over the moor to an appropriate viewpoint. If you don't want to do this, the road ahead leads to the parking area.

Leaving the guide stoop on Beeley Moor (Nov 12) **Top.** *Round-leaved sundew*

Hawthorn-time around Winster (May 26)

This ramble through an ancient mining landscape starts from the historic village of Winster with its old market hall and lead ore house; rises above the village for a fine panoramic view from Wyns Tor; wanders past the scheduled monument of the Beans and Bacon Mine (dating back to 1740) to Bonsall Mines and returns via The Limestone Way.

Length 11 kms/ 6.88 miles **Map** O/S Explorer OL 24 *White Peak Area*, East Sheet
Start/Finish A small car park at the head of the minor road that links the B5057 with the B5056 at SK 239 602. Winster is served by buses from Matlock and Bakewell. There is a bus stop beside Winster Hall at SK 240 625. Another CP is near the school on the B5057.
Terrain Paths and tracks across farmland and through ancient mine workings, where care is needed at some casually capped mineshafts. Route finding can be tricky in places with animal trails being misleading. There will almost certainly be animals in some fields.
Refreshments The *Bowling Green Inn* for walkers, *Miners' Standard* and village shop.
When To Go/What's There Winster itself has a fine church; hall, where recent renovations revealed unique frescos; 16th century market hall and lead ore house - a sort of miners bank where lead could be safely kept. The mine workings and ancient fields harbour a wealth of flora including fly, frog, pyramidal, fragrant, bee, early-purple and common spotted-orchids. Spring sandwort, thyme, kidney vetch, grass-of-Parnassus, field gentian, common restharrow, mountain pansy, lady's bedstraw, betony, cowslip, burnet saxifrage, milkwort, small scabious and common twayblade are among many other flowers. A wetland beside a path supports reedmace, spike rush, pondweed and water-crowfoot along with whirlygig beetles, water boatmen, pond skaters, frogs, newts, broad-bodied chaser and common darter dragonflies, and azure and large red damselflies. Birds include wheatear, red-legged partridge, skylark, redstart, lapwing and warblers. Brown hares flee and butterflies include common blue, gatekeeper, meadow brown and skippers.

The wetlands near Blakemere Lane. **Inset.** *Small scabious at Bonsall Mines (July 25).*

Left. *The broad-bodied chaser dragonfly breeds at the above wetland. From a painting of the male by the author (life size)*

Right. *Emerging from an adit at the Beans and Bacon Mine. Have a peep but don't enter; leave it to the cavers (May 9)*

Winster's old Market Hall

B5057 **Winster**

Limestone Way

Bonsall Lane

B5056

The ancient mining landscape (June 12)

north

* *Beans and Bacon Mine*

Upper Town

pool

Bonsall Mines

I————————I
1 km

Frog orchid (left) and pyramidal orchid with pollinator at the mines (July 25)

Route Turn left out of car park. Walk up to the **B5056**. Continue up left side of road then, opposite the *Lead Ore House*, turn left up track. After 300m turn right through stone stile. Go ½ left to wall stile and ½ left to another. Head leftish to gap/stile then head down left side of field to stile and road. Turn left. After 150m go through stile on right and cut ½ left to gap in wall. Then head to just right of the mound in next field to wall stile. Over, head ½ left to gate and lane. Turn right. After 200m turn left and bear right to pass left of conspicuous concrete-topped mound to track. Head up between fence and wall then follow wall on right to stile in wall. Head ½ left down field to stile in wall between hawthorns. Follow path through gorse to small ruins on left and waymark post on right. Up to the left is an adit of the ***Beans and Bacon Mine***. Return. Follow path through old wall and ahead down to wall corner. Through gap go on though another wall gap and diagonally down to corner of field and stile. Over, follow animal path down to corner of field where there is a hidden waymark post just left. Go through gap and down to gate/stile and track. Cross. Go through stile. Pass ***pool*** on right and follow isolated stile and waymark posts to track. Soon leave it on right (away from gate ahead) to wall stile. Through, keep ahead and pass through five old walls to wooden stile at small ruin. Don't go over, but double back on higher path up to waymark post. Go left up to wall corner. Go through gap and bear left. Just before barn on left bear right through gap and go up to another gap and fingerpost. Turn left. Cross double stile. Keep left of wall/fence to stiles in wall. Over, bear left to stile in wall and ahead over another stile and into ***Bonsall Mines***. Here, are paths through the old mine workings but return to this stile and, after 25m, go left through stile. You are now on ***The Limestone Way***, so follow the prominent path over fields/stiles to track. Go ahead down and, after 100m, turn left through stile beneath power lines. Follow path over fields, heading towards **Upper Town** in view, and down to road. Go up road ahead and stay on it as it hairpins right and leads to junction (well, post box). Turn left. At junction turn right then immediately go left through wall stile. Cross 3 fields to stile before barn. Through go left and follow wall on left. Keep ahead over 5 fields to track. Turn left. After 200m turn right through stile. Cross 6 fields to track. Turn right then immediately left through gate (not up track). Follow path through 5 fields/old walls to road. Turn left then right through gate. Follow path right of twin pylon to gate at wall corner. Through, and the way ahead runs pleasantly down fields (views inc Chatsworth) to wall. Bear left and follow wall on right to gate. Through, go left to gate and on path beneath *Luntor Rocks* and left of hummocks to gate. Go on to waymark post. Turn right down past old stone stile to gate and on through gap and then trees and old wall. Here, bear left to stile near houses at top of field. Take path between houses to lane. Go left uphill (or down to the *Bowling Green!*) and on to the car park.

Passing a capped mineshaft at Bonsall Mines

| 48 | Bow Wood, Riber, Dethick, Lea Gardens and Holloway |

Bluebells in Bow Wood (May 17)

After roaming through the woods, hills and fields of the Riber, Dethick and Lea area south-east of Matlock, you may wonder why this fine countryside was not included in the National Park. For gardeners, the walk passes very close to beautiful Lea Gardens.

Length 12 kms / 7.5 miles **Map** O/S Explorer OL 24 *White Peak Area*, East Sheet
Start/Finish Cromford Canal car park 2 kms south-east of Cromford on the Holloway road at SK 315 560. Local buses stop at the start of the walk proper (the entrance to Bow Wood) at SK 318 562. Ask for Lea Mill. Derbyshire buses 01298 23098.
Terrain An easy to follow route with most of the uphill at the start of the walk. Some of the paths can be muddy/slippery after rainfall. There is a little roadwork.
Refreshments Lea Gardens *café*; *Jug and Glass* at Lea (very short detours to both)
When To Go/What's There A walk for all seasons, but ideally go between early May to early June when the bluebells in Bow Wood are in flower and the dazzling array of rhododendrons bloom in Lea Gardens. There is an entrance fee to the gardens but the café, conveniences and plant sales are open to all. Riber Castle, which overlooks Matlock, is seen from Hearthstone Lane. St. John's church at Dethick was enlarged in 1530 by the Babington family, but the castellation is dated 1532. The tower is a favourite perch for singing yellowhammers, which you can enjoy whilst having lunch at the seat. Anthony Babington was beheaded after trying to free Mary, Queen of Scots. You glimpse *Lea Hurst*, the family home of Florence Nightingale; opposite is Lea Wood Hall. The original frontage of Riber Hall is passed. A farm on route offers soft fruit in summer. On the roadside back, there is a factory shop at Lea Mill. Buzzards soar above Bow Wood, stoats play in the farmland walls and brown hares the fields. When it snows you see how many animals there are by their tracks. There are some majestic old trees on route. Oxeye daisy, teasel, foxglove, hawkweeds, buttercup, red clover, knapweed, harebell, tormentil, wood sorrel, red campion and wild honeysuckle are some other flowers.

The path runs underneath the bow-shaped beech tree in Bow Wood (Oct 21)

In Lea Gardens at rhododendron-time (June 6). www.leagarden.co.uk

Riber

Riber Hall *

soft fruit *

I————————I
1 km

Lane

Carr

o *pond*

Hearthstone Lane

north

Bow Wood

to **Cromford**

factory shop *

P

bus stop *

Dethick

pond **0**

Jug & Glass *

Lea

Lea Gardens *

✝

Holloway

Long Lane

Lea Hurst *

Lea war memorial

Buzzards over Bow Wood

Through a winter wonderland at the start of Hearthstone Lane (Feb 4)

Route Walk up steps in car park and turn left on public footpath to road. Turn right. Follow pavement for about 300m then cross road and go through stile. Go ahead, not right, and walk up **Bow Wood**. After the bow itself (photo), keep ahead at X-paths to meet a lane. Turn right uphill and after 30m turn right (no f/p sign) off lane. Follow path through gates, always keeping ahead at junctions to top of **Hearthstone Lane** and down to Hearthstone Farm. After the buildings turn right onto a fenced-in path and onwards through two fields to a road (**Carr Lane**). Go up to junction. Turn right. 150m past ***Riber Hall*** entrance steps turn right over metal stile. Angle left to wall stile. Over, turn right down field to track. Go right and ahead to farm (seat). Go over stile left of buildings and ahead through fields and stiles to Carr Lane again. Turn left. Bear right at road junction. After about 350m, turn right down the track of **Wood Lane**. After 70m, turn left off track and follow fields/stiles ahead to road at **Dethick**. Cross. Walk ahead between buildings to church. Go through gate and down field to stile. Over, path forks. Bear right on path beside wall to stile. Over, follow path down wood; over footbridge and up steps to road. Turn right. After 40m (or 100 m to ***Jug & Glass***) cross road and go through gate and playground to another gate at lane. Cross lane and walk ahead up lane (left of *Post Office Cottages*). Keep ahead as lane becomes track. After 150m turn right down path which later becomes tunnel-like to meet lane (**Long Lane**). Right, 100m down lane is ***Lea Gardens*** but the route turns left. After 200m a gate gives access to the ***war memorial***. 200 m on, turn right down path. Follow down to lane. Bear left to road junction. Cross main road and go down Bracken Lane ahead. After 300m, at left bend, go over wall stile before house and down field to stile/gate on left. Here, turn 90° right. Soon there's a glimpse of ***Lea Hurst***, right. Cross drive, go through gate and bear left to wall stile. Follow path between deer fence/wall to field and its bottom right corner and to road. Turn left and follow roads down and on to start of walk.

Approaching Riber, with Riber Hall the building on the right (June 14)

Minning Low, Roystone Grange and Roystone Rocks

On the track to Roystone Grange (June 14)

This short, but most rewarding walk mainly follows the Roystone Grange Trail; but with new access land and concession paths now open we can also visit the haunting chambered tombs at Minning Low; a fine viewpoint and the mystical Roystone Rocks.

Length 7 kms / 4.38 miles **Map** O/S Explorer OL 24, *White Peak Area*, East Sheet
Start/Finish Minninglow car park; 1 km south of Pikehall off the A5012 and on the *High Peak Trail* at SK 194 581. There is no public transport.
Terrain An easy to follow walk on tracks, paths and lanes. There may be animals in some of the fields. It is uphill to Minning Low; the viewpoint and to Roystone Rocks.
Refreshments None
When To Go/What's There A pleasant stroll whatever the month; but is best enjoyed between June and August for the birds, flowers and insects. As with most granges in the White Peak, Roystone Grange was a monastic sheep farm. From the 12th-14th centuries it exported wool to Europe and beyond. Nearby is the shell of a 19th century pump house which provided compressed air to power the drills at many surrounding quarries. The area is archaeology rich with Romano-British settlements; ancient field systems; round cairns and the chambered tombs of Minning Low. Now down to fifteen, the beeches atop Minninglow Hill can be seen from a distance, including Stanage and Longstone Edges. The viewpoint summit rocks have *Xanthoria* and *Lecanora* lichens, biting stonecrop and fossils. There are early-purple orchids and cowslips amidst the dolomitic limestone arrays at Roystone Rocks. Minning Low has alpine clubmoss. Birds include curlew, skylark, wheatear and buzzards. Swallows nest in the open barns at Roystone Grange. There are rabbits, weasels and the odd daytime fox. Common blue, small copper, green-veined white, peacock and orange-tip butterflies enjoy other flowers including rock-rose, thyme, milkwort, knapweed, ox-eye daisy, hawkweeds, clovers, trefoils and St John's-wort.

Looking down on the old pump house from the viewpoint (June 14)

Passing a chambered tomb at Minning Low. **Inset.** *Common blue butterfly here.*

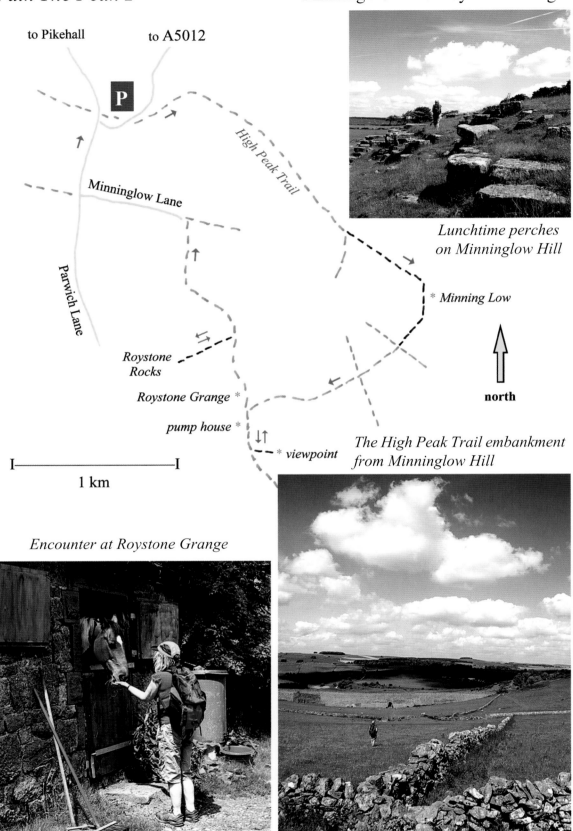

to Pikehall

to A5012

P

High Peak Trail

Minninglow Lane

Parwich Lane

*Lunchtime perches
on Minninglow Hill*

* Minning Low

north

Roystone
Rocks

Roystone Grange *

pump house *

* viewpoint

*The High Peak Trail embankment
from Minninglow Hill*

1 km

Encounter at Roystone Grange

Route Inside the car park walk west on the Pennine Bridleway; signed *Middleton Top*. After about 1½ kms; a cutting and an old quarry, turn left on the concession path to ***Minning Low*** (signed). Go through two gates; an old wall to a post and on up to the entrance. Walk through the site and out of the trees. Angle ½ right to waymark post and ahead to track. Cross. Go over wall stile and through tunnel beneath the ***High Peak Trail***. Head down field; through stile or wall opening to wall stile. Over, turn right down track to gate/stile, then go ½ left to stile. Turn left down metalled track. To see old ***pump house*** close-up and info board, go through gate on right and return. For ***viewpoint***, now go through left gate; walk down track and, where directed by post, turn left up the access land to the limestone knoll. Return to track. Turn right and follow track through ***Roystone Grange*** to a gate. About 60m on, to visit **Roystone Rocks**, turn left through gate (access signs) and head up field for a good walkabout. Return. Continue up track to gate and on to T-junction. Turn left on to **Minninglow Lane**. At X-roads turn right, and later first right again to the car park.

Top. *Minning Low in winter* **Below.** *Dolomitic limestone outcrops at Roystone Rocks*

Reading information boards at High Peak Junction (Nov 17)

A short walk visiting the historic mills (some optional) linked by canal, road and railway along what is now the Derwent Valley Heritage Way; designated a World Heritage Site.

Length 5 kms / 3.13 miles **Map** O/S Explorer OL 24, *White Peak Area*, East Sheet
Start/Finish Cromford Wharf car park and picnic site (with PCs) off the A6, ½ km east of Cromford at SK 300 570. Buses from Derby, Nottingham, Buxton, Manchester stop at Cromford Crossroads on the A6, where the route passes. Cromford station is ½ km away. Train information 08457 484950; bus information 0870 6082608
Terrain An easy to follow route on paths and tracks. The busy A6 has to be crossed via a convoluted pelican crossing system and care is needed at an interconnecting road.
Refreshments Cafés at Cromford Wharf, High Peak Junction, Arkwright's Mill, Scarthin and Cromford Crossroads. Chips in Cromford. The *Boat Inn* is muddy boot friendly!
When To Go/What's There Richard Arkwright built the world's first successful water powered cotton-spinning mill in Cromford over 230 years ago and lit the flame for such ventures worldwide. Small businesses now occupy the regenerated mill. Masson Mill is a shopping outlet with one business marketing many brands of whisky. The old waterwheel at the mill lake in Cromford village is in need of restoration. The incline upwards from High Peak Junction was a railed wagon line to lower quarried limestone from Middleton Top engine house to the Cromford Canal and onwards to the Midlands and elsewhere. The canal has matured into a local nature reserve but plans have been laid to restore the 15 miles of the canal to a navigable waterway. In the meantime, water vole, little grebe, kingfisher, pike, dragonfly and damselfly call it home. So do meadowsweet, flowering rush, hemp agrimony, pondweeds, umbellifers and associated butterflies and hoverflies.

Historic Masson Mill is now a shopping centre (300 metre detour)

Legendary Scarthin Books from across the mill lake (Nov 28). In the morning, a kingfisher currently hunts from the cypress tree on the left.

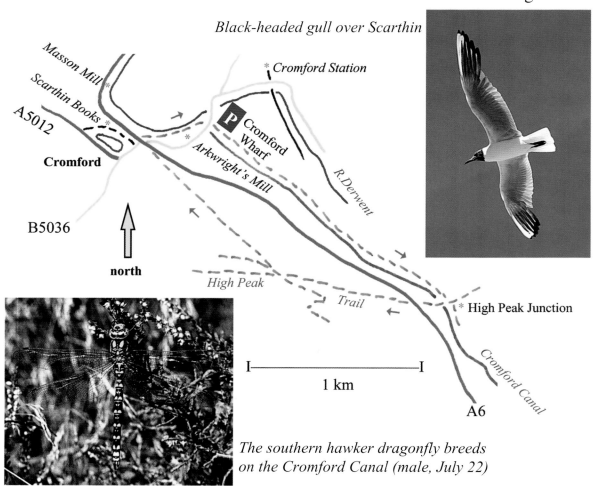

Black-headed gull over Scarthin

Masson Mill

Scarthin Books

A5012

Cromford

B5036

north

*Cromford Station

P Cromford Wharf

Arkwright's Mill

R.Derwent

High Peak

Trail

*High Peak Junction

Cromford Canal

A6

1 km

The southern hawker dragonfly breeds
on the Cromford Canal (male, July 22)

Strolling on the Derwent Valley Heritage Way in winter (Nov 28)

Route From the car parks walk to the canal at **Cromford Wharf** and turn left at the towpath. Follow it for about 1½ kms to **High Peak Junction** and cross the canal by the footbridge (sign High Peak Trail). Over, follow sign for *High Peak Trail*, passing rail wagons and winch wheel on left. Go through tunnel ahead under the **A6**. Pass the Catch Pit on the left. Here is where points were operated to divert runaway wagons away from workers below. Carry on up the incline (there's a steel sculpture on rocks opposite a tiny hut) for almost a km to finger post on left. Here, go up the steps left of old quarry (pulley systems) and follow path down to path junction and finger post. Turn left (signed *Cromford*) and go through tunnel beneath the path you were on (viewpoint, right). Follow track downhill. It becomes a side road (*Intake Lane*) and leads to the A6. Turn left and use pavement to traffic lights at X-roads. Turn left (signed *Cromford Village*). Cross **B5036** by pelican crossing (opposite *The Greyhound*) and turn left, then right up *Water Lane* on the **A5012**. After waterwheel on right, carefully cross road to *Cromford Garage* and turn right up *Scarthin*.

Pass (no, enter) unique **Scarthin Books** on the left and the *Boat Inn* on the right to rejoin the B5036. Turn left to a 4-stage pelican crossing to cross the A6 to *Tor Café*. Here, turn left then right, just before bus stop/shelter through gateposts on riverside path (if you opt to shop at *Masson Mill* follow A6 for another 300 metres or so). At end of crags on right a signed path leads to *Arkwright's Mill*. If you go, return and continue on the path through a gate right of St. Mary's Church. Cross the road ahead to the two car parks.

Small copper butterfly on hemp agrimony at the Cromford Canal

The riverside path at Cromford resembling an Impressionist painting (Nov 6)

51 Parwich, Ballidon, Bradbourne, Wibben Hill and Tissington

On the footbridge over Bradbourne Brook, adjacent to the vehicle ford (May 9)

Our final journey through The Peak starts in the fine village of Parwich; heads to an old chapel at Ballidon, then heads south to Bradbourne, with its Saxon cross, restored mill and ford. A gentle climb to Wibben Hill leads across the Tissington Trail to the tourist attractions at Tissington. From here, there is a final climb before descending to Parwich.

Length 11 kms / 6.88 miles **Map** O/S Explorer OL 24, *White Peak Area*, East Sheet
Start/Finish Car park in the village of Parwich at SK 189 542. Other car parks on route opposite Tissington Hall and on the Tissington Trail at SK 178 521. No public transport.
Terrain Predominantly farmland paths and tracks. There are a number of quite awkward stiles to negotiate. Many paths go through ridge and furrow fields. 3 kms are on lanes.
Refreshments Tea rooms at Tissington; *Sycamore Inn* at Parwich (with integral shop).
When To Go/What's There If you wish to view Tissington's famous dressed wells be prepared for huge crowds. The well-dressing festival is held on Ascension Day and lasts a week. The village also boasts a fine Jacobean manor house, home of the FitzHerbert family who also purchased Bradbourne flour mill in the 1900s. These 1750s buildings have been restored and twin waterwheels once more turn the millstones; however, for private eyes only! Opposite the mill is a popular vehicle ford with adjacent wetlands supporting marsh marigold, cuckooflower, marsh violet and large bitter-cress. Hares and, more rarely, a daytime fox roam the fields. Field flushes are visited by snipe; streams by grey wagtail and the skies by buzzard and skylark. There is a ninth century and much repaired shaft of a Saxon cross in Bradbourne churchyard. Other plants seen include field scabious, cowslip, bugle, early-purple orchid, ox-eye daisy, eyebright, hairy St. John's-wort, reedmace, clovers, trefoils, hawkweeds, harebell and knapweed.   *Field scabious*

Top Left. *Remains of the Saxon Cross in Bradbourne churchyard (Sept 2).* **Top Right.** *Looking down on cyclists on the Tissington Trail from the bridge over the trail on the way to Parwich.* **Above.** *Tissington Hall from Chapel Lane.* **Inset.** *Large bitter-cress (May 9).*

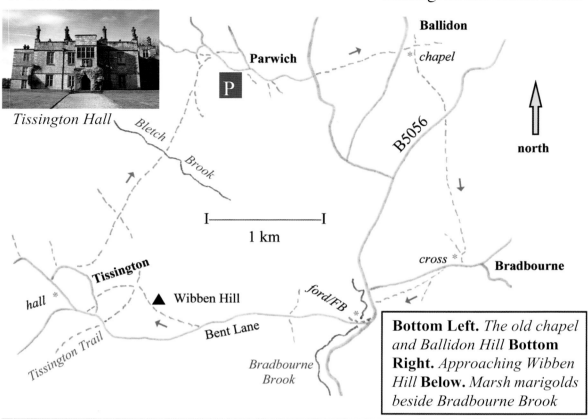

Tissington Hall

Bletch Brook

Parwich

P

Ballidon

*chapel

B5056

north

Tissington

hall *

▲ Wibben Hill

Tissington Trail

Bent Lane

ford/FB

cross *

Bradbourne

Bradbourne Brook

1 km

Bottom Left. *The old chapel and Ballidon Hill* **Bottom Right.** *Approaching Wibben Hill* **Below.** *Marsh marigolds beside Bradbourne Brook*

Route Turn right out of the car park. Left, note *Jubilee Stone* at pond. Pass junction on left to reach T-junction after ½ km. Cross road and go through stile right of gate. Follow hedge to stile on left; cross stream. Go ahead to stile in hedge. Head to right of wood ahead and cross stream. Head up left side of field to road. Turn left then right through stile. Head up to left of old ***chapel*** then turn right on track. Follow track. As it swings right to barn, keep ahead and follow hedge to road. Turn right then soon left over stile. Cross to stile ahead. Cross to right of tree where a pull handle gains access to field. Head right, aiming for just left of farm buildings and stile/gate. Go ahead to stile in hedge and cross stream. Ahead, cross another stream. Head over small field to stile. Over, head up field to stile in left corner. Head up through trees to enter churchyard left of church via stile and gate. Keep just left of church; pass Saxon ***cross*** and go ahead to road at **Bradbourne**. Turn right. After about 200m, turn left through stile. Bear right to stile(s) in wall. Through, go ahead (not left) to stile in hedge, right of track. Head down field to road. Turn left. Pass restored *Bradbourne Mill* on left then turn right down to ***ford***. Cross by footbridge and head up lane. After about 1½ kms, at the main entrance to *Bent Farm*, go through stile and head up field to left of the trees atop **Wibben Hill** and stile/gate in fence. The trig pillar is now up to the right. Through stile, angle a little right to gate in wall. Now angle ½ right over field to wall step-stile. Descend; cross ***Tissington Trail***; go up steps and cross field to gate/stile. Go ahead to stile/gate then left a little to gate. Through, turn right then left down lane and soon right again on footpath. Keep ahead to road; pass pond on left then turn right. Pass *Tea Rooms* and ***hall*** on left (*Hall Well* on right) then turn right (wall sign for *Sawpit Hill*) up Chapel Lane. At junction bear left on Flatts Lane. Ahead, cross bridge over *Tissington Trail* then, half-way round left bend turn right, signed to **Parwich**. Head down field; go over wall step-stile and on to stile left of short wall. Over, walk on to cross ***Bletch Brook*** by footbridge. Head up steep field to stile/plank through hedge. Keep right of hedge; go through stile/gate and then ahead by hedge to stile. Descend path to stile. Over, keep ahead (not right) down to stile. Through, immediately turn right; pass through stile and follow path beside stream and ahead to road; *Sycamore Inn* on left and car park ahead.

Taking the path from Tissington to Parwich, with Minning Low on the horizon, right of centre (June 13)

Four More Tops

There are four hills well worth ascending that were unable to be included in either of the two volumes. But if you're in the area and have an hour or so to kill then these tops, all now on access land, are recommended :

1 Wolfscote Hill

The wonderful limestone outcrops beneath the summit of Wolfscote Hill (April 5)

Map O/S Explorer OL24 *White Peak Area* West Sheet

Location Trig Pillar at SK 137 583

Start There is no public transport so park at the end of Beresford Lane which is two kms south of Hartington at SK 127 586

Route Cross the River Dove by the footbridge then head left up to a path, above the one through the meadow. Keep ahead as the path crosses a track, soon to meet a lane. Turn right and, just after Wolfscote Grange, a gate on the left gives access to the hill. There is currently new fencing in progress but there should be openings to allow the top to be gained.

The Trig Pillar sits atop a huge tumulus where excavations revealed a stone cist containing the skeletons of two children.

2 Gun

Looking to Shutlingsloe above the trig pillar on Gun (May 4)

Map O/S Explorer OL24 *White Peak Area* West Sheet **Location** Trig pillar at SJ 970 615
Start No public transport. There is parking for a few cars where the public footpath to Gun
starts from the minor road, 3 kms west of Meerbrook at SJ 967 609. **Route** An easy ¾ km
stroll over moors to the trig pillar. Only 27m height to gain! **What's There** The final few
steps to the pillar reveal the views to Ramshaw Rocks, The Roaches, Hen Cloud,
Tittesworth Reservoir, Shutlingsloe and Jodrell Bank radio telescope on the Cheshire Plain.
The houses around Meerbrook exhibit their "scarecrow" creations May Day Bank Holiday.
Tittesworth Reservoir has bird hides, walks and refreshments.

3 Wardlow Hay Cop This top could be tagged onto Walk 39 of *Walk The Peak*

Through the wood anemones to the trig pillar on Wardlow Hay Cop (May 1)

Map O/S Explorer 24 *White Peak Are*a East Sheet
Location Trig Pillar at SK 178 739 Start Public footpath on the west side of the B6465 between Monsal Head and Wardlow Mires at Wardlow: SK 181 745. There is no public transport. Roadside parking but there is a small lay-by a few metres north on the east side of the road. **Route** If you have *WTP* you could tag this on to Walk 39. If not, follow path and after the second stile go ½ left on path to wall corner. Here, go 90° left and follow wall on the left uphill for about 400m to gates on left. Through, your quarry is in sight. But walk out opposite gate to see view first. **What's There** If you head due west on the way back, there is a weather station. From here, bear right to the access gate. Although grazed, in early May the entire hill is carpeted with wood anemones. There are also a few mountain pansies, cowslips and early-purple orchids. In summer, the hill blooms with yellow rattle, small scabious, harebell, dwarf thistle, trefoils, clovers and milkwort. There are extensive views to The Great Ridge with Kinder Scout beyond, Bretton, South Head, The Tors above the Goyt Valley, Longstone Edge, Stanage Edge, Monsal Head, Fin Cop and Minning Low.

Dwarf thistle near the trig pillar (July 30)

4 Eccles Pike

Map O/S Explorer 01 *Dark Peak Area* West Sheet

Location Toposcope at SK 035 812. It is only a short walk uphill from a small parking area at the top of Eccles Road which is equidistant from Whaley Bridge and Chapel-en-le Frith.

What's There This a fine viewpoint from a relatively low peak - the hills being identified by a rather different toposcope than is normally encountered. Chinley Churn (Walk 13), Kinder Scout, Sponds Hill (seen from Walk 14) and Combs Edge and Reservoir (Walk 24, *WTP*) are among the most prominent. In summer the gorse houses linnets, hoverflies and gatekeeper butterflies.

Left. *Looking out from the unique toposcope on Eccles Pike.*

Below. *On the short (200m) path up to the summit of Eccles Pike. It is fortunately National Trust land.*

A Few Extra Scenes

As this volume has a shorter **Introduction** than *Walk The Peak* there are a few spare pages to include some photos that didn't feature in the walk sections of either volume :

A barrel of geese at Blackwell Cottages (Walk 28)

Pyramidal Thorpe Cloud from Ilam Hall (Walk 40, Oct 18)

Howden Dam towers seen from the drive to walks in the upper Derwent (Nov 15)

Parapenters on Rushup Edge (Walk 24, Feb 27). See what they did on page 116.

It was hard to capture the sense of exposure on Giddy Edge (Walk 48, WTP , June 10) ...

... but easy to capture the desolation on Bleaklow! (Walk 6, WTP , Aug 19)

Unusual Mileposts

Whilst on our travels through the parish of Bradfield in South Yorkshire, we came across a number of unique milestones. Some have vernacular spelling or original names of the villages such as *Wightwizzle* for *Wigtwizzle* as is on the O/S map (Dark Peak). A few are pictured here. See page 92 for another.

Also in the area is a *Take-off Stone*, situated on the opposite side of the road and 30m north of the *Strines Inn* at SK 222 906. A take-off stone was a stone instructing the coachman to unhitch the extra horse needed to pull a coach up a steep hill. In this instance, the climb up from Strines Bridge.

Top Left. *Bolsterstone Road T-junction, just east of Swanheight at SK 272 942*

Top Right. *Crossroads near Peat Pits Farm at SK 277 938*

Left. *Crossroads south of White Lee Farm at SK 269 949*

More on the web at *Yorkshire Milestones; Region South Yorkshire; Sub-region Bradfield*

St Helen's Church graveyard, Darley Dale, after the heavy snow of 2 December 2010

The sculptures on Paine's Bridge, Chatsworth (WTP, Walk 43, Oct 17)

Shutlingsloe from near Bottom-of-the-Oven (Dec 3)

Derwent Edge from Ladybower Reservoir (Dec 27)

Looking to Rushup Edge from Mam Tor (Jan 9)

The start of the ascent of Kinder Scout via Fair Brook (Walk 7, WTP, March 6).
Fairbrook Naze is in snow, right of centre. The River Ashop is in the foreground.

Crook Hill taken from opposite Heatherdene car park (WTP, Walk 18, July 29)

Fairbrook Naze, Kinder Scout, from the Woodlands Valley (Oct 25)

Approaching Derwent Reservoir from the path above Abbey Brook (Walk 16, WTP)

On the lane to Glutton Bridge (Walk 28, WTP, Dec 29)

When the going gets tough ... the sensible turn round and go home! (Labouring through a snow-choked Pennine Way on Bleaklow, winter 2009)

On the valley path through the beautiful Upper Derwent (referred to in Walk 13, WTP)

When Derwent Dam is overflowing, it's a good bet that the spillway shafts (formerly called spillage holes) of Ladybower Reservoir will be, too (April 4, 2010)

Seasonally Clad Pubs Top. *The Eyre Arms at Hassop in autumn attire (close to Walk 43, Sept 18).* **Bottom.** *The Cat & Fiddle on the A537 above Buxton is the Peak District's highest pub, but it can be tricky to get to in winter! (New Year's Day 2010)*

Frozen pool beside Goyt's Lane, on the way to many walks in this area (Jan 4)

Igloo-building at a frozen Blake Mere (Walk 33, Jan 2)

Wife crossing a frozen and windswept Big Moor (Feb 14: a Valentine's Day treat?)

This sunset by Shutlingsloe was taken on April 2 at 19.47 - the day and year of my birth!

References

Barnatt, J. and Robinson, F. (2003) Prehistoric Rock-Art at Ashover School and Further New Discoveries Elsewhere in The Peak District. *Derbyshire Archaeological Journal* **123** : 1-28.

Cunningham, P. (Landmark, 2006) *Peakland Air Crashes (The North)* pp 60; 135

Useful Web Sites/Phone Numbers

For public tranport go to www.traveline.org.uk Enter the time and date of travel, your start location and destination - nearest village/town - and the site will lay out your route. You can also print relevant bus/train timetables.

National Train Enquiries 08457 484950; Bus Traveline 0870 608 2608

Open Access Contact Centre (for when access land may be closed) 0845 100 3298

Peak District National Park Office 01629 816200

Errata *Walk The Peak*

In *Disclaimer* line 3 for "you" read "your"

Page 20 Line 5 for "beehiveshaped" read "beehive-shaped"

Page 58 On map add "Dale" to "Alport"

Page 59 Line 19. The 5 stepping stones have been dispersed. The path down Hern Clough starts about 20 metres south of a stone waymark post at GPS Ref SK 09706 94790.

Page 102 bottom line. There is more *Defiant* wreckage than I found. Cunningham (2006) quotes most remains at SK 15286 90495. See above.

Page 116 delete "(*see p.24*)" from map

Page 118 In "Start/Finish" the A625 has been re-routed. CP now beside unclassified road.

Page 119 in "Top Right". Lose Hill was purchased by the Sheffield and District Federation of the Ramblers Association in appreciation of the pioneering "right to roam" work of George Herbert 'Bert' Ward and the hill was also christened *Ward's Piece*. It was later presented to the National Trust. My comment was somewhat erroneous.

Page 167 bottom line for "*The Black Swan*" read "*The Black Lion*" (sorry landlord, must have had one too many!)

Acknowledgements

I would like to thank: Joe and Ian at Clocktower Computers, Chesterfield for saving the book data from both volumes after motherboard crashes; CJWT Solutions, St Helens for converting both volumes to commercial printing; Pete Woolhouse for being great company as we enjoyed adventures on the walks and for proof-reading the script; Jen Shimwell for sharing her knowledge of Rowarth and Old Glossop; Chris Boyd, Will and Sarah Waites for their companionship and willingness to be rucksack models; David Shimwell for identifying some wild flowers; Robin Jones for determining some fungi; Brian Woodall for information on the limestone ore-crushing ring on Eldon Hill; and my family: Brenda, Reece and Susie who again walked all weather without a grumble and also greatly assisted in the production of the manuscript. Dave Mitchell and his team of David Booker (Publishing Manager), Guy and Wendy Cooper at Scarthin Books were again enthusiastic and supportive.

We only have one life and we owe it to ourselves to enjoy it and be as free-spirited as possible in this troubled world. As I have enjoyed many wonderful experiences, I therefore dedicate this volume to my late mother and father, who gave me life. *Carpe diem!*

Rod Dunn has been walking, climbing and conducting environmental surveys in The Peak District for over 35 years. He has also climbed extensively in the Alps, Dolomites and Tyrol and ascended all the major European peaks. In 1969 he was in the first party to successfully walk the Peak District National Park from north to south in under 24 hours. In 1982 he co-founded *The British Dragonfly Society*. His 24-year survey of *Dragonflies in Derbyshire* was published in 2005. An anthology of his illustrated verse, *Aerosol Dreams*, was published in 1975. *Walk The Peak* was published in 2007. His roots are firmly in the Peak District: his mother's line descends from the *Fox House Inn* near Grindleford, and his father's from the *Belle Vue Hotel*, Tideswell (now a private residence). Born in Bakewell, he was educated at Lady Manners and lives in Darley Dale.

The author lay-backing "Cordite Crack" at Lawrencefield Quarry, above Hathersage

photo credit : Phil Lewis

About a sixth of the photographs for this volume were taken on a Nikon F65 fitted with a Nikkor 28-100 mm lens and using Fujichrome Sensia 100 slide film. Dents of Chesterfield scanned the slides to CD. This camera set-up was blown over on a tripod once too often and smashed. My son then dragged me into the digital age by buying me a Canon EOS 400D, to which I attached a Canon EFS 17-85 mm lens. Film or digital? Err, well ...

… *"Oh lay me down in moorland ground*
And make it my last bed,
With the heathery wilderness around
And the bonny lark o'erhead;
Let fern and ling around me cling
And green moss o'er me creep,
And the sweet wild mountain breezes sing
Above my slumbers deep."

- **Edwin Waugh**
(The Moorland Breeze 1889)